The Divine Mandates

The Divine Mandates

MORRIS A. INCH

WIPF & STOCK · Eugene, Oregon

THE DIVINE MANDATES

Copyright © 2017 Morris A. Inch. All rights reserved. Except for brief quotations in critical publications or reviews, no part of this book may be reproduced in any manner without prior written permission from the publisher. Write: Permissions, Wipf and Stock Publishers, 199 W. 8th Ave., Suite 3, Eugene, OR 97401.

Wipf & Stock
An Imprint of Wipf and Stock Publishers
199 W. 8th Ave., Suite 3
Eugene, OR 97401

www.wipfandstock.com

PAPERBACK ISBN: 978-1-4982-8435-6
HARDCOVER ISBN: 978-1-4982-8437-0
EBOOK ISBN: 978-1-4982-8436-3

Manufactured in the U.S.A.   JANUARY 12, 2017

Contents

Preface | vii

Realm of Divine Mandates | 1

Prophetic Times | 13

Prophecy Fulfilled | 28

Apostolic Fathers | 40

The Apologist | 52

Cost & Command | 64

Labor Mandate | 75

Family Mandate | 87

Government Mandate | 98

Church Mandate | 110

Life | 122

Liberty | 134

Pursuit of Happiness | 146

All Things Considered | 157

Bibliography | 167

Preface

TWO RIVAL ANALOGIES COMPETE for our attention: the law of the jungle and a sacred canopy. As for the former, life consists of the survival of the fittest. As an invitation to materialism and tyranny.

As for the latter, the divine mandates serve as a framework for social enterprise. In keeping with the notion that we live in God's world, and by his grace. For the purpose of his glory, resulting in our individual and corporate blessing.

The extended discussion explores the topic in greater detail. Initially, with the realm of mandate. What is its nature? As such, what do mandates share in common? How do they structure life? Expressly as reflected in the Mosaic Covenant and that with Noah. As if a means of bringing order out of chaos, recalling how God managed concerning the natural world. And now in context of our social relationships.

Then, in turn, with what is described as *the paper trail*. Which consists of a brief survey, providing a context for the divine mandates. First by way of exploring the Old and New Testaments. Subsequently, with the apostolic fathers, discourse of the apologist, and an interlude with Dietrich Bonhoeffer. The last of these serves a marked transition into a discussion of the mandates in greater detail while the entries combine to serve as a credible reality check.

The traditional mandates are four in number: As regards the church, family, government, and labor. It amount to a short list, since other options readily come to mind. So while not exhaustive, they provide a valuable framework for casting life in context of the divine mandates.

Although not as a rule discussed in connection with the divine mandate, the notion of endowments is critically relevant. In terms of our bill of rights, they are said to consist of life, liberty, and the pursuit of happiness.

Preface

The sanctity of life being indispensably foundational for the remainder. Liberty being a logical extension, and the pursuit of happiness offering an opportunity but not serving as a guarantee.

All things considered serves to summarize the extended discussion in terms of the divine mandates. "You are the light of the world," Jesus informed his disciples. "A city on a hill cannot be hidden. Neither do people light a lamp; and place it under a bowl. Instead they put it on its stand, and it gives light to everyone in the house. In the same way praise your Father in heaven" (Matt. 5:14-16).

Several observations appear strikingly pertinent. First, faith is associated with its social context, rather than in strict isolation. Allowing for the fact that both solitude and social engagement are contributing features. "Each by itself has profound pitfalls and perils. One who wants fellowship without solitude plunges into the void of words and feelings, and one who seeks solitude without fellowship perishes in the abyss of vanity, self-infatuation, and despair." [1]

The divine mandates thus serve in a dual capacity. Obviously, in establishing the credential of select social institutions, but also by insisting that persons comply with legitimate social obligations. Consequently, requiring accountability from those who exercise authority and those subject to it.

Second, so as to solicit praise for the Heavenly Father. With whom life originates in all its multi-faceted benefits. In matters great and small, momentary and lingering. While allowing for the fact that it unravels if not lived according to God's righteous guidelines.

Instead of courting the approval of others. Recalling that genuine humility is not given to either pride or self-effacement. Since the latter amounts to a negative expression of pride, as unduly dwelling on self. But rather, *to God be the glory*; since great things he has done and continues to do.

Finally, as implied above, there is the existential feature of life. "When I consider your heavens, the work of your fingers, what is man that you are mindful of him," the psalmist reflects. "You make him a little lower than the heavenly beings and crowned him with glory and honor" (Psa. 8:3-5).

Meant to superintend God's creation, humans continue to fall short of their appointed task. So that creation suffers as a result, as do humans as well. Along with the diminishing of God's glory. Calling for a commitment of the divine mandates, seeing that we are at fault in this regard, with disastrous effects by commensurate promise

---

1. Dietrich Bonhoeffer, *Life Together*, p.78.

Realm of Divine Mandates

THE DECALOGUE SERVES TO introduce the realm of divine mandates. Its importance can hardly be overstated. The rabbis "speculated that it was prepared on the eve of creation in anticipation of subsequent use; they asserted as each commandment was sounded from the lofty height of Sinai it filled the world with a pleasing aroma; they concluded that all nature hushed to hear every word as it was spoken.[1]

The *ten words* are apodictic in character, rather than specific instances. In other words, they constitute broad general principles. For instance, "You shall not murder" (Exod. 20:13). As over against, "If men who are fighting hit a pregnant woman and she gives birth prematurely, but there is no serious injury, the offender must be fined whatever the woman's husband demands and the court allows. But if there is a serious injury, you are to take life for life, eye for eye," etc. (Exod. 21:22–24).

The context of the Decalogue follows the pattern of a vassal treaty. In which the *Sovereign Lord* pledges to intercede on behalf of his chosen people on condition of their faithful observance of the covenant provisions. Initially, the Suzerain announced: "I am the Lord your God, who brought you up out of Egypt, out of the land of slavery." Hence, deserving of their resolute faithfulness.

"You shall have no other gods before me." "Thus the first 'word' takes aim at atheism (we must have a God), idolatry (we must have Yahweh as our God), polytheism (we must have the Lord God alone), and formalism (we must live, fear, and serve the Lord with all our heart, soul and strength,

---

1. Inch, *Scripture As Story*, 35.

The Divine Mandates

and mind. The ground of all morality begins here"[2] Consequently, *before me* implies that we should not allow for other deities, regardless of their subordinate rank.

If not acceptable to God, then to whom? Either as a consensus, or imposed by those in authority. Which is calculated to serve invested interests. As such, unworthy to be considered as a credible ethic.

"You shall not make for yourself an idol in the form of anything in heaven above or on the earth beneath or in the waters below" as a logical progression. "You shall not bow down to them or worship them; for I the Lord your God, am a jealous God, punishing the children for the sin of the fathers to the third and fourth generation of those who hate me, but showing love to a thousand generations of those who love me and keep my commandments."

It goes without saying that *anything* is comprehensive. So when a human agenda is given prime importance, it amounts to idolatry. Recalling the sage observation, "It is not the blatant evil we do, but the lesser good that more likely threatens the greater good."

The rabbis also reasoned that we should take the greatest of care not to give the impression that we engaged in idolatry. So it was that they counseled that should one drop money before an idol, he or she should turn away before picking it up. They reasoned further that even a legitimate effort to recover their funds might adversely condition them. While this may seem unlikely, it reveals how seriously they endorsed the prohibition.

"The accompanying rationale recognizes the social implications of our actions. That is, whatever we do or fail to do impacts on others. Even so, God promises to restrain evil influence which cultivating the good we do.[3] So that while living in a fallen world is not the best of situations, neither is it the worst.

"You shall not misuse the name of the Lord your God, for the Lord will not hold anyone guiltless who misuses his name." Negatively, this precludes taking the name of God casually, hypocritically, or for magical purposes. Initially, one much not employ God's name thoughtlessly. As is a habitual practice, void of significance.

Nor in hypocritical fashion. "And when you pray, do not be like the hypocrites," Jesus admonished his disciples, "for they love to pray standing in the synagogues and on the street corners to be seen by men" (Matt.

---

2. Kaiser Jr., *Toward Old Testament Ethics*, 85.
3. Inch, *Scripture as Story*, 36.

6:5). They have their reward, such as it is; but lack any reason for divine commendation.

Nor for magical purposes. Since magic entails the idea that we can manipulate the powers that be. As such, it not only disarms the Almighty, but is essentially void of moral considerations.

Positively considered, one is to employ God's name reverently, lovingly, and earnestly. Reverently, because God is both great and good. As sovereign, he is deserving of our respect. As benefactor, he is worthy of our appreciation.

Lovingly, in response to God's love extended to his fallen creatures. Giving rise to C.S. Lewis' observation that because God loves us, he endeavors to make us lovable. Serving as a gracious initiative with which we should heartily cooperate.

Earnestly, as one striving for excellence. Do you not know that in a race all the runners run, but only one gets the prize"?" Paul rhetorically inquires. "Run in such a way as to get the prize" (I Cor. 9:24). Which requires strict training in preparation, and vigorous execution.

"Remember the Sabbath day by keeping it holy. Six days you shall labor and do all your work, but the seventh day is a Sabbath to the Lord your God. On it you shall not do any work, neither you, nor your son or daughter, nor your manservant of maidservant, nor your animals, nor the alien within your gates." Out of deference to the Almighty, and a reminder of the critical role he plays in Life's equation.

This admonition recalls how God had rested from his creative activity, thus setting a precedent (cf. Gen. 2:2–3). So that in Jewish tradition it precluded anything that might be thought analogous. Such as preparing food, although partaking of food is said to be especially enjoyable in context of the Sabbath celebration.

It was not generally understood that those other than the chosen people were obligated to observe the Sabbath, unless associated with them. Certain rabbis allowed that it was optional. If of intrinsic value, it would seem to be at least permissible. If only a distinctive feature of a select community, then not obligatory.

Thus concludes the first segment of the Decalogue, focusing on the relationship between God and the covenant community. Consisting of singular worship, refraining from the use of idols, prohibition of using God's name in vain, and the Sabbath observance. Giving the impression that

The Divine Mandates

Idolatry would be a continuing temptation that must be strictly rejected. So that the rabbis reason it is the source for evil in its multi-faceted expression.

The second segment addresses the tenuous relationship among humans. As a logical extension of the previous injunctions. In this regard, "If anyone says, 'I love God,' yet hates his brother, he is a liar, for anyone who does not love his brother, whom he has seen, cannot love God whom he has not seen. And he has given us this command, 'Whoever loves God must also love his brother'" (I John 4:19-21).

"Honor your father and your mother, so that you may live long in the land the Lord your God is giving you." This consists of respect, obedience, and meeting their needs, especially during their declining years. First, respect of one's parents. Since they with God were involved in giving birth, and each has a legitimate invested interest.

Moreover, the rearing of children is a formidable undertaking. Near constant attention early on, and with lingering obligations. Not that parents are without fault, but neither can they be blamed for all that goes wrong It is not simply the circumstances, but how we respond to them that determines the outcome.

While bearing in mind that God as a rule employs imperfect means to achieve his gracious purposes. So that we ought not to demean such as serves his agenda. Nor the parents' willingness to comply, qualifications notwithstanding.

Second, through obedience. Allowing for the fact that they are more knowledgeable. Along with the realization that what we do or fail to do impacts others. Accordingly, in keeping with their calling as parents.

Obedience extends beyond reluctant compliance to a ready acceptance. Such as is exhibited in the positive attitude we cultivate. While extending to related matters, thought consistent with our obligation.

This is calculated to stand one in good stead as he or she matures. When no longer expected to inquire of one's parents for their direction, but faithfully applying their teaching to subsequent developments. In other words, making decisions consistent with one's upbringing.

Finally, in taking care of one's parents. Not only concerning their physical needs, but social and spiritual as well. In characteristically progressing fashion, as the need increases along with the means to meet it.

Then, when the parents have passed on, to appreciatively remember them and their service. As when one puts flowers on the grave, or simply recalling some pleasant event from the past. As a sage reminder, "gone but not forgotten."

"You shall not murder." That is, to take one's life without due cause. Which assumes that there is justification, and that the means is authorized. It also allows for a distinction between premeditated and accidental behavior.

Undergirding this prohibition is the sanctity of life, as a divine provision. Giving rise to what is identified as *the old absolute*, as set over against *the new absolute*. As for the former, "Human Life from conception to natural death is sacred and worthy of protection." In greater detail, "The Lord gave and the Lord has taken away; may the name of the Lord be praised" (Job 1:21). As for the latter, "Human life, which begins and ends when certain individuals or groups decide it does, is valuable as long as it is wanted."[4]

Recalling John Calvin's observation that if one can save a life, and fails to do so, he or she has committed murder. Since sins of omission are no more acceptable than sins of commission. Thus leaving persons with difficult decisions concerning the preservation of life, and the risk involved.

"You shall not commit adultery." While insisting on marital fidelity, this prohibition was thought to extend to a wide variant of unacceptable sexual behavior. For instance, "No one is to approach any close relative to have sexual relations" (Lev. 18:6). As another, "Do not lie with a man as one lies with a woman" (18:22). And still another, "Do not have sexual relations with an animal and defile yourself with it: (18:23).

In conclusion, "Keep my requirements and do not follow any of the detestable customs that were practiced before you came and do not defile yourselves with then. I am the Lord your God" (18:30). As otherwise expressed. "Do not conform any longer to the pattern of this world, but be transformed by the renewing of your mind. Then you will be able to test and approve what God's will is; his good, pleasing and perfect will: (Rom. 12:2). In both instances, persons are enjoined not to continue an unacceptable practice that characterizes the prevailing culture.

Instead, to be *transformed* by the renewing of one's *mind*. Having dwelt on the prophetic word, embrace it. Along with the expectation that this will result in a radical departure from previous ways of thinking and behavior. So likewise convinced that this is not only for the better but without exception the best of alternatives.

---

4. Watkins, *The New Absolutes*, 65.

"You shall not steal." "According to rabbinic tradition, one is guilty whether he or she brazenly robs in public or in secret; whether in taking possession from another or kidnapping the person; whether involving much or little; whether outright or with usury; whether concerning property or reputation."[5]

In a peasant society, where the margin for survival is minimal, any theft might result in hardship, if not in death. In a covenant community, theft, no matter how otherwise serious, was an affront to God and a denial of life together. Recalling the satirical comments, "What is mine is mine, and what is his is mine as well."

Theft can be of personal or of corporate nature. As the former, it need not pertain to material possessions, but anything rightly belonging to another. Such as demeaning one's character or intent. As for the latter, excessive taxation amounts to corporate greed and theft.

"You shall not give false testimony against your neighbor." The seriousness of this prohibition can be seen in that it could result in his or her death. If not, then in lesser punishment. Neither of which was acceptable in a covenant community.

Persons are admonished to tell the truth, the whole truth, an nothing but the truth. The *truth* in contrast to what is false. If such occurred, report it as having happened. If not, do not pretend that it transpired. When much or little is at stake.

The *whole truth* without which it is distorted. Which allows for extenuating circumstances. Along with accounting for differences of perception. As a means of reconciliation, where this is feasible. And justice. Regardless of outcome.

Nothing but the truth so not to introduce unrelated matters. Thereby to divorce truth from its essential context. Whether with intent or lack of discipline. In keeping with Augustine's provocative comment, "All truth is God's truth."

"You shall not covet your neighbor's house. You shall not covet your neighbor's wife, or his manservant or maidservant, his ox or his donkey or anything that is your neighbor's." "*House* means 'household', in the early sense of the word, and the thought of 'wife' is primary. *Ox* and *ass* are the typical wealth of the bronze age peasant or semi-nomad, for whom the

---

5. Inch, *Scripture as Story,* 37.

perplexities of developed society have not yet arisen. 'Slaves are the only other form of movable property.'[6]

This final interdict makes explicit what has been implicit up to this point: our predatory desires give rise to our perverse practices. Recalling the vivid contrast mentioned at the outset between the law of the jungle and sacred canopy. As for the former, where those most fit survive. As for the latter, where life is celebrated as God's benevolent design, and lived out according to his righteous instructions.

"When people saw the thunder and lightning and heard the trumpet and saw the mountain in smoke, they trembled with fear. They stayed at a distance and said to Moses, 'Speak to us yourself and we will listen. But do not have God speak to us or we will die.'" Thus were they overwhelmed with God manifesting his presence among them.

"Do not be afraid," Moses encouraged them. "God has come to test you, so that the fear of God will be with you to keep you from sinning." So that the awesome impression of this event would be passed down from one generation to the next, as a cherished but solemn legacy.

At this juncture, the text turns from general principles to select instances (cf. 21:1). As an example: "Anyone who strikes a man and kills him shall surely be put to death. However, if he does not do it intentionally, but God lets it happen, he is to flee to a place I will designate. But if a man schemes and kills another man deliberately, take him away from my altar and put to death" (21:12–14).

The vassal treaty concludes with a warning should the chosen people fail to keep their covenant obligations, a promise of blessing should they do so, and the prospect of covenant renewal. In the first instance, "The Levites shall recite to all the people of Israel in a loud voice: 'Cursed is the man who carves an image or casts a idol—a thing detestable to the Lord, the craftsman's hands—and sets it up in secret'" (Deut. 27:15). *In secret* presumably because this seemed more acceptable than in public.

"Then all the people shall say, 'Amen!'" Thus voicing their hearty agreement that this is unacceptable and calculated to result in calamity.

In like manner, "Cursed is the man who dishonors his father and his mother." Again soliciting a favorable response from the populace.

By way of contrast, should they obey the Lord: "You will be blessed in the city and blessed in the country. The fruit of your womb will be blessed,

---

6. 7. Cole, *Exodus*, 161.

and the crops of your land and the young of your livestock. You will be blessed when you come in and blessed when you go out."

Thus recalling the motif of two ways: that of the righteous and that of the wicked. As for the former, "Blessed is the man who does not walk in the counsel of the wicked or stand in the way of sinners or sit in the seat of scorners" (Psa. 1:1). Implying a progression from bad to worse. "But his delight is in the laws of the Lord, and on his law he meditates day and night." Such resemble trees planted having ready access to water.

"Not so the wicked! They are like chaff that the wind blows away." Without root or substance. At the mercy of the elements.

Two ways, no more or no less. There is no neutral ground. But there is an option. So choose well!

There remains the provision for covenant renewal (cf. Deut. 29), which anticipates both change and continuity. Change to accommodate different circumstances, as when the chosen people took up resident in the promised land. Continuity with the covenant principles. Soliciting the sage observation, "The more some things change, the more other things appear constant."

Here we take leave of the Mosaic Covenant, to consider God's covenant with Noah—as concerns the Gentiles. Which was thought to be a renewal or extension of his original covenant with Adam. In particular, "Adam taught his children the Seven Universal Laws: not to worship idols, not to curse God, not to kill, not to steal, not to engage in sexual immorality, not to eat the limb of a living animal, and to establish courts of law to enforce these laws."[7]

Concerning idolatry. The essence of the *Seven Universal Laws* is said to be the prohibition against idolatry. This pertains to any aspect of creation. Nothing in the natural world around us: neither plants or animals, neither terrestrial nor celestial, neither individual or groups. Not that which we produce: whether a material object or appealing ideology, whether for a fleeting moment or extended time, whether or not approved by others.

A person may learn from his or her observations without falling prey to idolatry. For instance, the sage enjoins: "Go to the ants you sluggard, consider its ways and be wise!" (Prov. 6:6). Recalling a time as a child I intently watched ants scurrying back and forth. Not only was I impressed by their industry, but their seemingly cooperative endeavor.

---

7. Clorfene and Togalsky, *The Path of the Righteous Gentile*, 8.

Realm of Divine Mandates

The Jewish tradition was not uniform concerning whether it is permissible to believe that other gods exist, so long as one does not worship them. Some thought this was acceptable, while others rejected the notion. Abraham serves as an example, in that commentators disagree as to whether he allowed for the existence of other gods, while agreed that he was committed to Yahweh.

There was also conjecture as to whether persons were obligated to lay down their lives rather than compromise their convictions. While permission to do so was readily granted. Resulting in some ambiguity at this point.

In any case, persons are warned not to delve into idolatry—lest led astray. One's interest might pick up in the process. Accordingly, Jesus taught his disciples to petition: "And lead us not into temptation, but deliver us from the evil one" (Matt. 6:13). Idolatry being a prime example.

Concerning blasphemy. "Are you still holding on to your integrity?" Job's wife incredulously inquired of him. "Curse God and die!" (Job 2:9)

"You are talking like a foolish woman," the patriarch replied. "Shall we accept good from God, and not trouble?" Soliciting the commendation, "In all this, Job did not sin in what he said."

Blasphemy was thought to fall into the category of revenge. "When someone is harmed by a person and seeks revenge, he may shout at the person or curse him. If the harm is great, the one seeking vengeance may not be satisfied by words alone but may physically strike out at the one who harmed him. In extreme cases, the vengeful person may not be satisfied till he kills."[8]

Such is vengeance among humans. The situation differs concerning God. Whereas humans cannot physically assault the Almighty, let alone kill him; they can only express their hostility. Consequently, blasphemy is viewed with the intent to hurt God, even to erase his existence.

Blasphemy expresses itself most vividly when humans attribute evil to God . Recalling the faulty reason of an acquaintance, who protested: "If God gave me a mind, and I conclude that he does not exist, he is at fault." Not unlike Adam, who excused his transgression with the observation: "The woman you put here with me—she gave me some fruit from the tree, and I ate it (Gen. 3:12).

In more subtle fashion, blasphemy was thought involved whenever one fails to give God the recognition due him. Whether this pertains to his

---

8. Ibid., 74.

sovereign authority, or his benevolent design. Consequently, by challenging the assertion that God is good, and does good.

Concerning murder. In this connection, "Whoever sheds the blood of man, by man shall his blood be shed; for in the image of God has God made man" (Gen 9:6). Not only is murder a disregard for the sanctity of life, but an affront to God—in whose image man is created.

The implications are extensive. For instance, "Abortion of a fetus, even in the most sophisticated of ancient societies, was a health risk for the mother. For this reason, the author believes that the Old Testament is concerned with the practice of infant sacrifice, which might be considered the Canaanite counterpart to abortion."[9]

Or should a person leave someone to starve, it was said to constitute murder. Assuming that he has available means or could secure it to save the person's life. Again, emphasizing the culpability of sins of omission.

If death occurred unintentionally, the perpetrator was to be provided security. Since retaliation might be expected. Bringing to mind the sage counsel, "Two wrongs do not made a right."

Concerning theft. Of all the commandments, the prohibition against theft was thought the most difficult to obey. Largely because one is inclined to further his or her own interests at the expense of others. And then to justify the abhorrent behavior in some acceptable manner.

One was liable to punishment whether he or she brazenly robs in public, or sneaks into a house under the cover of darkness. Regardless from whim one steals, or the amount taken. As when failing to provide a reasonable wage. Whether deliberately or not recognizing the implications.

In Talmudic times, a fair amount of profit was thought to be one-sixth. However, it was allowed that the percentage would have to be adjusted occasionally, while weighing in the contributing factors. Falling prey to man's predatory nature.

The prohibition against theft was best served by not coveting that which belongs to another. Instead, rejoice in his good fortune. And seek to emulate his industry, while being generous to a fault.

Concerning sexual immorality. "For this reason a man will leave his father and mother and be united to his wife, and they will become one flesh" (Gen. 2:23). "In antiquity, parents arranged marriages at significant financial cost, and the groom's parents might easily have thought that they had authority over their son despite the marriage. Therefore the son must

---

9. Hoffmeier, "Abortion and the Old Testament Law," 53.

Realm of Divine Mandates

leave his parent in order to break the authority line to them, and honor his wife as is true counterpart, the central person in his life."[10]

Sexual purity was to be maintained in this context. As a commitment, for better and for worse. Until life's termination. Not begrudgingly but with hearty approval, as unto the Lord.

Divorce, although discouraged, was allowed in more exceptional instances. Resulting in a wide range of application. In some instances, restricted to adultery and in others for less compelling reasons.

It was thought that those involved in illicit sex would eventually come to realize the folly of their behavior, and complain against those who encouraged them. Once they realize the risks involved, and its meager compensation.

Concerning forbidden food. "Everything that lives and moves will be food for you," the Lord allowed. "But you must not eat meat that has its lifeblood still in it" (Gen. 9:3-4). Explicit in this prohibition is partaking of a living animal. Implicit is the notion of humane treatment. In brief, "Animals, birds, and fish may be killed for food in any way that man deems to be efficient and it should be done as humanely as possible."[11]

Such as violated by the crowded condition to which animals are subject. Moreover, the crude slaughtering procedures so often employed. Not only with concern for the animals, but its adverse effect on the humans involved.

By way of extension, showing consideration for all forms of life. The beasts of the field, the birds overhead, and the foliage surrounding us. As a good steward of God's creation, rather than a ravaging plague.

Concerning courts of law. Such as further the cause of justice, and cultivate moral behavior. As a deterrent to evil, and a means of cultivating a healthy society. As a task of prime importance, to be zealously pursued.

Worthy of note, the *lex talionis* (an eye for an eye) was meant to discourage extreme forms of punishment. Conversely, it allowed for extenuating circumstances. By which justice is served.

The provision for courts of law allowed for variety. Providing this was deemed in keeping with basic moral principles. So that while what constituted modesty might legitimately differ from one culture to the next, a concern for modest behavior ought to prevail regardless of cultural distinctive.

---

10. Hartley, *Genesis*, 63.
11. Clorfene and Rogalsky, *The Path of the Righteous Gentile*, 98.

The Divine Mandates

There were many factors to bear in mind. For instance, the judge should not assume the merits of the case on the basis of the good or bad reputation of one of the litigants. Since either or both might be at fault.

Nor should the judge unnecessarily delay the proceedings, by lengthening the time of testimony or cross-examination. Such as calculated to increase the distress of those implicated. While serving no legitimate purpose.

Thus have we explored the realm of divine mandates. First concerning the Mosaic Covenant and then God's covenant with Noah. As for the former, said to set forth 613 regulations, but reduced to 7 in the latter instance. Although the latter are for the most part more general, and thought to be roughly equivalent. While focusing our attention on man's relationship to the Sovereign Lord, and life together.

Prophetic Times

From the beginning. Scripture begins with the solemn affirmation, "In the beginning God" (Gen. 1:1). We are thus alerted to the fact that at the outset God stands alone in solitary splendor. There is no rival. No, not one!

The religious pantheon was a later addition, meant to serve human caprice. Along the line of human fiction

Initially, the earth was *formless and void*. Resembling the amorphous clay cast by a potter, before fashioning a vessel—both functional and aesthetically pleasing. It was a barren landscape, lacking life. Now the Spirit of God was hovering over the waters, in anticipation of the task that lay ahead.

"Let there be light," God declared, "and there was light." And God was that it was good. Then in other regards, concluding with the observation: "God saw all that he had made, and it was very good."

"By way of implications, man was born free, with the intent that he should remain free. Not free from obligation, which is license, but free to cultivate a relationship with God and one another."[1] So things would have remained had he abided by God's instructions.

Instead, he ate from the forbidden fruit. Our choices either open new opportunities, or further restrict those we previously enjoyed. This proved to be no exception. Life took a decided turn for the worse, for the original couple and their posterity. For instance, Adam was informed: "Cursed is the ground because of you; through painful toil you will eat of it all the days of your life" (Gen. 3:17).

---

1. Inch, *Scripture as Story*, 18.

Worthy of note, even small changes in original conditions are calculated to have disproportionate results. Moreover, this was a defection of major proportions. Leaving the impression that Life was radically altered.

By way of a reality check, Eve gave birth to two sons: Cain and Abel. In the course of time, Abel offered fat portions from the firstborn of his flock to the Lord, as one would honor a distinguished guest. While Cain offered a token alternative. Consequently, God Looked with favor on Abel's offering, but with manifest disfavor on his brother's sacrifice.

"Why are you angry?" the Lord inquired of Cain. "If you do what is right, will you not be accepted? But if you do not do what is right, sin is crouching at your door; it desires to have you, but you must master it" (Gen. 4:6–7). Sin is thus depicted as a predatory animal, waiting to devour its victim. If not vanquished, it will succeed.

Cain nonetheless proposed to his brother, "Let's go out to the field." Arriving at a secluded place, he attacked and killed Abel. And then refused to assume responsibility for his despicable behavior.

"What have you done?" God exclaimed. "Listen! Your brother's blood cries out to me from the ground. Now you are under a curse and driven from the ground, which opened its mouth to receive your brother's blood from your hand. When you work the ground it will no longer yield its crops for you. You will be a restless wanderer on the earth." "It was believed that uncovered human blood cried out for vengeance against the murderer. If no one heard the cry, God was obligated to redress the wrong."[2]

Some time later, Lamech informed his wives: "I have killed a man for wounding me, a young man for injuring me. If Cain is avenged seven times, then Lamech seventy-seven times" (Gen. 4:23–24). Thus revealing the swift progress of sin, by way of contrasting the impulsive behavior of Cain with the calculated retaliation of his vengeful successor.

Matters continued to deteriorate. Now the Lord saw how great the wickedness of man had become, how "that every inclination of the thoughts of his heart was only evil all the time" (Gen. 6:15). One could hardly imagine a more scathing indictment.

So the Lord determined to bring a flood upon the earth, as if to cleanse it from its contamination. As might a potter, when he sees that his work in progress I compromised, starts over. With the prospect of better success.

Even so, Noah found favor in the eyes of the Lord. He "was a righteous man, blameless among the people of his time, and he walked with God."

---

2. Hartley, *Genesis*, 83.

So the Lord warned him of the impending disaster, and instructed him to build an ark for the deliverance of his family and perpetuation of the human race.

In retrospect, "By faith Noah, when warned about things not yet seen, in holy fear built an ark to save his family. By his faith he condemned the world and became heir of the righteousness that comes by faith" (Heb. 11:7). As illustrative of the thesis, "Now faith is being sure of what we hope for and certain of what we do not see" (v 1).

Once the waters had receded, God covenanted with Noah. Recalling the earlier discussion of its features. By way of exploring the character of the divine mandates.

Now the whole world had a common language. As men moved eastward, they found an inviting plain in Shinar and settled there. "Come, let's make bricks and bake them thoroughly," they admonished one another. "Come, let us build ourselves a city, with a tower that reaches to the heavens, so that we may make a name for ourselves and not be scattered over the face of the whole earth" (Gen. 11:3–4)

"The elements of the story are timelessly characteristic of the spirit of the world. The project is typically grandiose; men describe it excitedly to one another as if it were the ultimate achievement—very much as modern man glorifies in his space projects."[3] Their expressed purpose being to *make a name for ourselves,* and provide security within the confines of their habitation.

Appraising the situation, the Lord decided to confuse their language, so as to discourage their presumption. This resulted in their aborting the effort, and being scattered throughout the world. Recalling the observation, "From one man he made every nation of men, that they should inhabit the whole earth, and he determined the times set for them and the exact places where they should live. God did this so that men would seek him and perhaps reach out for him and find him, though he is not far from each one of us" (Acts 17:26–27).

With the patriarchs. It was said of the patriarchs that while they were men of faith, they were not always faithful. It is perhaps for this reason that it seems so easy to identify with them. In any case, they constituted a new phase in salvation history.

The Lord instructed Abram, "Leave your country, your people and your father's household and go to the land I will show you" (Gen. 12:1).

---

3. Derek Kidner, *Genesis,* 109.

The prospect was not inviting on two counts. First, he was to take leave of familiar surroundings, and the security and sense of belonging associated wit his *people* and *father's household*. Second, he would be thrust into an alien environ, along with uncertainties and potential risks these involved.

Conversely, "I will make you a great nation and I will bless you; I will make your name great, and you will be a blessing. I will bless those who bless you, and whoever curses you I will curse; and all peoples on earth will be blessed through you." He would be blessed in the process, protected from his adversaries, and become the means of universal blessing.

"So Abram left," in obedience to God's directive. He "traveled through the land as far as the site of the great tree of Moreh at Shechem. At that time the Canaanites were in the land." This was presumably a sacred tree, in keeping with the practice of traditional people—in this instance, the *Canaanite*.

The Lord appeared to Abram, and informed him: "To your offspring I will give this land." So Abram erected an altar at that location. After which, he continued on to Bethel, and again built an altar. Thus laying claim to God's promise.

The word of the Lord subsequently came to the patriarch, "Do not be afraid, Abram. I am your shield, your very great reward" (Gen. 15:1). "The negative imperative appears here and on other occasions, as with Isaac (26:24) and Jacob (46:3). With the passing of time, it came to serve as formula for encouragement, having been tested and not found wanting. As elaborated the *shield* implies his protection, and *great reward* his provision.[4]

Some time later God again addressed Abraham (Abram). "Take your son, your only son, Isaac, whom you love and go to the region of Moriah," the Lord instructed him. "Sacrifice him there as a burnt offering on one of the mountains I will tell you about" (Gen. 22;2). In retrospect, "Abraham reasoned that God could raise the dead, and figuratively speaking, he did receive Isaac back from death" (Heb. 11:19).

As the patriarch reached for his knife to slay his son, an angel protested: "Do not do anything to him. Now I know that you fear God, because you have not withheld from me your son. Your only son." Abraham looked up and saw a ram caught by its horns in a thicket. Accordingly, he sacrificed the ram instead of his prized offspring.

---

4. Inch, *Scripture as Story*, 26.

"So Abraham called the place The Lord Will Provide. And to this day it is said, 'On the mountain of the Lord it will be provided.'" In anticipation that God would make provision for those who put their trust in him.

Now Isaac's wife Rebekah gave birth to twin boys: Esau and Jacob. The former became a skilled hunter, while the latter was more retiring. Once when Jacob was cooking stew, his brother came in from the open country. "Quick, let me have some of that red stew!" he exclaimed. "I'm famished!" (Gen. 25:30).

Jacob replied, "First sell me your birthright." "The firstborn received a larger portion of the inheritance; according to Deuteronomy 21:17, the firstborn received a double share. Jacob, the master manipulator, perceived that Esau was too exhausted to value something as abstract as birthright over tangible food at the moment."[5] Moreover, one gets the impression that he had been anticipating such an opportunity.

"Look, I am about to die." Isaac protested. "What good is the birthright to me?" So he sold his birthright under oath to his sibling. Soliciting the critical comment, "So Esau despised his birthright."

Fearing for his life, Jacob fled to his uncle Laban. When he had reached a certain place, he stopped for the night. He had a dream in which he saw a stairway resting on the earth, with its top reaching to heaven, and angels ascending and descending on it. There above it stood the Lord, who declared: "I am the Lord, the God of your father Abraham and the God of Isaac. I will give you and your descendents the land on which you are lying. I am with you and will watch over you wherever you go, and I will bring you back to this land" (Gen. 28:13, 15).

So the patriarchal period continued to run its course. Employing manifestly imperfect means to achieve God's redemptive purposes. While in different circumstances, drawing from a righteous resolve.

With the exodus. Now the Israelites fled famine to Egypt, where they remained for an extended time. A new king, unfamiliar with Joseph, who enjoyed a cordial relationship with those in authority, ascended the throne. So that he was less amenable to their tenuous situation. "Look," he alerted the populace, "we must deal shrewdly with them or they will become even more numerous and, if war breaks out, will join our enemies, fight against us and leave the country" (Exod. 1:9–10).

So he put slave masters over them to oppress them with forced labor. But the more they were oppressed, the more they multiplied and spread.

---

5. Hartley, *Genesis*, 237.

The Divine Mandates

Then the ruler instructed some helping Hebrew women who gave birth to kill the male offspring. But the midwives feared God, and excused their failure to comply. Then Pharaoh set forth a public proclamation, insisting; "Every boy that is born you must throw into the Nile, but let every girl live." With the intention that the latter would be assimilated. Which amounted to genocide.

"Now a man of the house of Levi married a Levite woman, and she became pregnant and gave birth to a son. When she saw that he was a fine child, she hid him for three months" (Exod. 2:1–2). When she could hide him no longer, she placed the child in a papyrus basket and put it among the reeds. His sister stood at a distance to see what would transpire.

When Pharaoh's daughter went down to the Nile to bathe, she saw the basket and had one of her servants retrieve it. Seeing the crying child, she felt sorry for him. Enlisting the help of his sister to recruit a Hebrew woman (His mother) to nurse the child, she adopted him when older. She named him *Moses*, derived from the verb meaning to pull out.

One day, when Moses had matured, he saw an Egyptian beating *one of his own people*. Assuring himself that there was no one watching, he killed the oppressor and hid his body in the sand. When Pharaoh heard of this, he determined to have Moses killed. But the he fled to Midian to escape Pharaoh's wrath.

There he married and was tending the flock of his father-in-law when he saw a burning bush that was not consumed. "What actually did Moses see: Was it a supernatural vision or was it an actual physical phenomenon? If the latter, did he see a bramble bush literally blazing in the desert; or the shrub called 'burning bush', in brilliant flower; or the sunset light falling full on a thorn bush and producing the effect of flames?[6] All of these alternatives have been suggested.

In any case, he heard a voice from the bush cautioning him: "Do not come any closer. Take off your sandals, for the place where you are standing is holy ground." Then the voice continued, "I am the Lord the God of your father, the God of Abraham, the God of Isaac and the God of Jacob" (Exod. 3:5–6). In other words, the God the patriarchs.

The Lord then assured him, "I have indeed seen the misery of my people in Egypt. I have heard them crying out because of their slave drivers, and I am concerned about their suffering. So I have come down to rescue them from the hand of the Egyptians and to bring them out of that

---

6. Cole, *Exodus*, 64.

land into a good and spacious land, a land flowing with mild and honey." Hence, ideal from a pastoral perspective. "So, now, go. I am sending you to Pharaoh to bring my people the Israelites out of Egypt."

When Moses protested his lack of credentials, God assured him: "I will be with you. And this will be a sign that it is I who have sent you: When you have brought the people out of Egypt, you will worship God on this mountain." Initially, this recalls the saying: "One with God is in the majority." Subsequently, "The proof of the pudding is in its eating."

Afterward, Moses and Aaron went before Pharaoh, and informed him: "This is what the Lord, the God of Israel says, 'Let my people go, so that they may hold a festival to me in the desert'" (Exod. 5:1). Consequently, even rulers are subject to God's sovereign authority.

"Why are you taking the people away from their labor?" Pharaoh indignantly replied. Then he instructed his slave drivers, "Make the work harder for the men so that they keep working and pay no attention to lies." Which incited Moses to complain to the Lord for worsening the situation, with no relief in sight.

The stage was set for a series of plagues to descent on Egypt. Some "have suggested that a sequence of natural occurrences can explain the plagues, all originating from an overflooding of (the Nile). Those who maintain such a position will still sometimes admit to the miraculous nature of the plagues in terms of timing, discrimination between Egyptians and Israelites, prior announcement and severity."[7] With the exception of the tenth plague, concerning the death of the firstborn. Not that we lack answers, but seen at a loss to ask the appropriate questions.

Pharaoh finally relented, only to have a change of mind. Pursuing the Israelites, his forces perished when the waters which parted to let the Israelites pass, returned to engulf their pursuers. An event perhaps associated with volcanic activity in the Aegean region.

So it was that the Israelites were able to covenant with God in the wilderness. Since we explored this topic earlier, we need not expand on it further. They remained to possess the promised land.

With the conquest. "See, the Lord your God has given you the land," Moses declared to the populace. "Go up and take possession of it as the Lord, the God of your fathers told you. Do not be afraid; do not be discouraged" (Deut. 1:21). But the people were reluctant to comply, and asked that

---

7. Walton and Matthews, *Genesis-Deuteronomy,* 91–92.

spies be sent ahead, to bring back word as to what they might expect. The suggestion seemed to have merit, and so Moses did as they requested.

The spies subsequently reported that it was indeed a good land. However, "The people are stronger and taller than we are; the cities are large, with walls up to the sky. We even saw the Anakites there." The *Anakim* were said to be giants. So that the people refused to lay hold of God's promise and possess the land. "We have sinned against the Lord," the Israelites eventually concluded. "We will go up and fight, as the Lord our God commanded us."

It was too late, because God had withdrawn his approval from this generation. Nonetheless, the people insisted, and were soundly defeated. It remains for "every generation of God's people to avoid such a chain reaction: you were unwilling . . . you rebelled . . . you were afraid . . . you saw but . . . you did not trust . . . you thought it easy . . . you would not listen . . . you rebelled . . . you came back . . . you wept . . . you stayed."[8]

The *midbar* (wilderness) was an uninviting prospect. Life was exceedingly difficult, and survival threatened. The people complained. The food was not to their liking. They questioned the wisdom of their leaders. They were inclined to blame others for their misfortune. One generation passed and a new generation replaced it.

After the death of Moses, *the servant of the Lord*, the Lord said to Joshua: "Now then, you and all these people, get ready to cross the Jordan River into the land I am about to give to them. I will give you every place where you set your foot, as I promised Moses" (Josh. 1:2–30. "God points Joshua and the tribes toward the potential gift, the Fertile Crescent, the part of the Middle East that reaches across the northern Syrian Desert and extents from the Nile Valley to the Tigris and Euphrates rivers. The tribes will need to wait until the reign of David to achieve anything near to those borders."[9]

Joshua subsequently instructed the populace, "When you see the ark of the covenant of the Lord your God, and the priests, who are the Levites, carrying it, you are to move out from your positions and follow it" (Josh. 3:3). After which, he admonished them: "Consecrate yourselves, for tomorrow the Lord will do amazing things among you." Although the Jordan River was at flood stage, when the priests' feet touched the water's edge, the water from upstream stopped flowing—allowing the Israelites to pass over into the promised land.

8. Wright, *Deuteronomy*, 52.
9. Harris et al., *Joshua, Judges, Ruth*, 18.

Prophetic Times

"From a geographical perspective, the Jordan River Valley lies at the juncture of tectonic plates that create an unstable region. Earthquakes occur and have been known to block the flow of the river."[10] However explained, this qualified as one of the *amazing things* they were to witness.

Another consisted in the collapse of the walls of Jericho. The people were instructed to march around the city's wall once for six days. "On the seventh day, march around the city seven times, with the priests blowing the trumpets. When you have them sound a long blast on the trumpets, have all the people give a loud shout: then the all of the city will collapse and the people will go up" (Josh. 6:4–5). So it came to pass, providing a foothold for the Israelites within the promised land.

The struggle intensified. Sometimes with favorable results, and on other occasions with disaster. Consequently, the Israelites were able to settle in the land, while many of its inhabitants yet remained. This was in keeping with the promise that they would possess *every place you set your foot*.

With the monarchy. The turbulent time of the judges served as a transition into the era of the monarchy. It consisted of a predictable pattern: the people would succumb to sin, call out to God in their desperation, be delivered, enjoy peace for a time, only to fall back into their sinful ways. "The type of leadership that judges provided was unique to the ancient Near East. They were charismatic figures, divinely raised up in times of crises from outside the traditional power circles to meet a specific threat, namely, oppression."[11] An exception did not prove to be the rule.

Now when Samuel was well advanced in years, he appointed his sons as judges. However, they "did not walk in his ways. They turned aside after dishonest gain and accepted bribes and perverted justice" (1 Sam. 8:3). So all the elders protested: "You are old, and your sons do not walk in your ways; now appoint a king to lead us, such as all the other nations have." While their concern was justified, looking to *all the other nations* as a model suggests that they hoped to embrace a contemporary cultural pattern rather than seeking God's will. "The unreconciled ambiguity found in the attitude toward kingship throughout its somewhat questionable history is reflected. On the one hand, kingship could be seen as a rejection of God's own kingship. On the other hand, it was a gift from God, a model and a

---

10. Hess, *Joshua*, 104–105.
11. Harris et al., *Joshua, Judges, Ruth*, 123.

The Divine Mandates

channel through which God's relationship with Israel could be illustrated and strengthened."[12]

Consequently, God counseled Samuel: "Now listen to them, but warm them solemnly and let them know what the king who will reign over them will do." In greater detail, "He will take your sons and make them serve with his chariots and horses, and they will run in front of his chariots. Some he will assign to be commanders of thousands and others of fifties, and others plow the ground and reap his harvest, and still others to make weapons of war."

But the elders insisted, "We want a king over us. Then we will be like all the other nations, with a king to lead us and to go out before us and fight our battles." Without regard for their unique calling as the chosen people, and in this capacity, to serve as a light to the Gentiles.

Samuel subsequently summoned the people of Israel before the Lord at Mizpah, to anoint a ruler over them. "We cannot be sure how the lottery took place. But the indication of God's choice through the drawing of lots is fairly common throughout Scripture and various, sometimes now obscure, methods being used. The king is appointed from among the people and, whatever powers he might be assigned, he remains one of them."[13]

In any case, Saul appears as a likely candidate. He was from the relatively small tribe of Benjamin, and so should not fuel controversy among the major clans. He was also "an impressive young man without equal among the Israelites—a head taller than any of the others" (1 Sam. 9:2), and appealingly humble (9:21, 10:22). As a matter of record, the rulers of the united monarchy had an auspicious beginning, while falling away with the passing of time. David's record would remain the least tarnished, due in large measure to his deep sense of contrition.

The monarchy consisted of an intricate system of checks and balances. There was the *king*. Qualifications aside, if he observed the covenant stipulations, the people would prosper. If not, they would suffer along with him. In brief, like ruler, like people.

There were the *prophets*. Whose monumental task was to fine-tune the people to their covenant commitment. "What manner of man is the prophet?" Abraham Heschel rhetorically inquires. "To us a single act of injustice—cheating in business, exploitation of the poor—is slight; to the prophets, a disaster. To us injustice is injurious to the welfare of the people;

---

12. Evans, *1 and 2 Samuel*, 41–42.
13. Ibid., 50.

to the prophets it is a deathblow to existence; to us, an episode, to the, a catastrophe, a threat to the world."[14]

There were the *priests*. Such provided meaningful ritual for worship purposes. While accenting God's holiness and righteous resolve. As a reminder of the human proclivity to sin, and as a summons to repentance and faith.

There were the *sages*. Who were more perceptive than the general populace. As a result, more skilled in engaging life. Some of whom acted in an official capacity to lend guidance to royalty. Others qualified as an elder. In ideal terms, as extended to parents in their privileged role in guiding their offspring.

Finally, there were the *people*. Without their consent, the efforts of those in authority would be fruitless. Without their participation, the task would be impossible, recalling the sage advice, "One for all, and all for one."

David was subsequently informed "Your house and your kingdom will endure forever before me; your throne will be established forever (2 Sam. 7:16). *Forever* would evolve into the anticipation of a Messiah, from the lineage of David.

"How great you are, O Sovereign Lord!" David exclaims. There is no one like you, and there is no God but you. And who is like your people Israel—the one nation on earth that God went out to redeem as a people for himself. You have established your people forever, and you, o lord, have become their God."

The Lord appeared to Solomon in a dream, and invited him: "Ask whatever you want me to give you" (1 Kings 3:5).

"Now, O Lord my God, you have made your servant king in place of my father David," Solomon allowed. "But I am only a little child and do not know how to carry out my duties. So give your servant a discerning heart to govern your people and to distinguish between right and wrong.?

This greatly pleased the Lord, so that he replied: "I will give you a wise and discerning heart, so that there will never have been anyone like you, nor will there ever be. Moreover, I will give you what you have not asked for—both riches and honor." And so it came to pass, only to have Solomon violate his covenant obligations. Along with the ominous warning that this would eventuate with the division of the kingdom.

With the exile. So it was that Jeroboam rebelled against Solomon, and fled to Egypt until the latter's demise. He then, along with *the whole*

---

14. Heschel, *The Prophets*, 4.

assembly of Israel, approached Rehoboam with the observation: "Your father put a heavy yoke on us, but now lighten the harsh labor and heavy yoke he put on us, and we will serve your" (1 Kings 12:4).

Rehoboam rejected the advice of the elders who had served his father, in favor of young men of his age. "My father made your yoke heavy; I will make it heavier," he stridently replied. "My father scourged you with whips; I will scourge you with scorpions."

When *all Israel* saw that the king refused to heed their request, they inquired: "What share do we have in David, what part is Jesse's son? To your tents, O Israel! Look after your own house, O David!" And so the kingdom was rent in two.

With little exception, Israel would remain impervious to the pleas of the prophets. It plunged headlong into destruction, which eventuated in the fall of Samaria to the Assyrians. As if caught in a tight spiral, from which there was not recovery.

The Southern Kingdom fared better, benefitting from periodic spiritual renewals. For instance, Josiah "went up to the temple of the Lord with the men of Judah, the people of Jerusalem, the priests and the prophets—all of the people from the Covenant, which had been found in the temple of the Lord" (2 Kings 23:2). For the purpose of renewing the covenant. "then all the people pledged themselves to the covenant."

His efforts notwithstanding, Judah's days were numbered. Jehoahaz did evil in the eyes of the Lord (cf. 23:32), as did Jehoiakim (cf. 24:9), and Zedekiah (cf. 24:19). As an evil legacy passed on from one reign to the next. So it came to pass that the Babylonians lay siege to Jerusalem. Then the city wall was broken through. Every important building was burned to the ground. Including the temple and palace. And so the people were taken a way into captivity, leaving behind some of the poorest people to work the vineyards and fields.

Resulting in an imaginative reconstruction: "The caravan had made its way up the slopes of the Trans-Jordan Plateau. From there it would travel along the King's Highway toward Damascus and eventually Babylon. The column paused long enough to look back toward Jerusalem. The torched city was bellowing smoke into the air."[15] The captives wondered what the future held with the City of the Great King devastated, and the temple complex destroyed.

---

15. Inch, *Scripture as Story*, 85.

Prophetic Times

As for apt commentary, "Almost all the old symbol systems had been rendered useless. Almost all the old institutions no longer functioned. What kind of future was possible for a people who had so alienated their God that categorical rejection was his necessary response?"[16]

"By the rivers of Babylon we sat and wept when we remembered Zion," the experience of exile is painfully recalled (Psa. 137:1). "Our captors asked us for songs, our tormentors demanded songs of joy; they said, 'Sing us one of the songs of Zion!' How can we sing the songs of the Lord while in a foreign land?" How indeed!

"If I forget you, O Jerusalem, may my right hand forget its skill. May my tongue cling to the roof of my mouth if I do not remember you, if I do not consider Jerusalem my highest joy." As for the Edomites, who applauded the efforts of the Babylonians, recall their transgression. As for the Babylonians, retribution awaits.

The prophets, who had warned of impending judgment, now turned their attention to comforting the exiles with the prospect of their return. With such in mind, Cyrus issued a proclamation which read: "The Lord, the God of heaven, has given me all the kingdoms of the earth and he has appointed me to build a temple for him at Jerusalem in Judah. Anyone of his people among you—may his God be with him, and let him go up to Jerusalem in Judah and build the temple of the Lord, the God of Israel, the God who is in Jerusalem" (Ezra 1"2–3). While urging their neighbors to contribute the means to accomplish this demanding enterprise. Thus the exile draws to a close.

With "the second exodus." The return from exile has been graphically described as *the second exodus*. Since those returning anticipated reclaiming the land of promise. Along with a renewal of their covenant, eventuating in God's blessing.

"When the seventh month came and the Israelites had settled in their towns, the people assembled as one man in Jerusalem. Despite their fear of the peoples around them, they built the altar on its foundation and sacrificed burnt offerings on it to the Lord, both the morning and evening sacrifices" (Ezra 3:1, 3). Their common cause providing encouragement in spite of opposition.

When the foundation of the temple was laid, the priests and Levites sang: "He is good; his love for Israel endures forever." "But many of the older priests and Levites and family heads, who had seen the former temple wept

---

16. Klein, *Israel in Exile*, 3.

aloud when they saw the foundation of this temple being laid, while many others shouted for joy. No one could distinguish the sound of the shouts of joy from the sound of weeping, because the people made so much noise." While not comparable to the splendor of the former edifice, it marked a significant beginning.

Although delayed, the temple was completed. "Then the people of Israel—the priests, the Levites and the rest of the exiles—celebrated the dedication of the house of God with joy" (Ezra 6:16). Extensive sacrifices were offered. They also installed the priests in their divisions and the Levites in their groups for the service of God, and celebrated the Passover.

It was brought to Ezra's attention that the "people of Israel, including the priests and Levites, have not kept themselves separate from the neighboring peoples with their detestable practices" (Ezra 9:1). Upon hearing this, he tore his tunic and cloak, pulled hair from his head and beard, and sat down appalled at the situation. Then everyone who *trembled at the words of the God of Israel* joined him.

A proclamation was subsequently sent throughout Judah for all the exiles to assemble in Jerusalem. "Anyone who failed to appear within three days would forfeit all his property, in accordance with he decision of the officials and elders, and would himself be expelled from the assembly of the exiles" (Ezra 10:8). It was a decisive action meant to deal with a critical issue.

When the people assembled, Ezra declared: "You have been unfaithful; you have married foreign women, adding to Israel's guilt. Now make confession to the Lord, the God your fathers, and do his will." Rather than heartily embracing their role as a chosen people, set apart for God's service.

"You are right!" the people exclaimed. "We must do as you say." Opposition was minimal (cf. v. 15).

"Comparatively few had availed themselves of the opportunity either then or on later occasions, and sixty years later large numbers of Jews remained in the eastern half of the Persian empire, many in the great imperial cities of Persia itself."[17] While little is known of them, the text of Esther provides an interesting insight.

"Now the king was attracted to Esther more than to any of the other women, and she won his favor and approval more than any of the other virgins. So he set a royal crown on her head and made her queen" (Esther

---

17. Baldwin, *Esther*, 17.

2:17). He was not aware of her Israelite identity, nor did she volunteer the information.

Given the opportunity to intercede on behalf of her oppressed people, she made the most of it. "On this day the enemies of the Jews had hoped to overpower them, but the tables were turned and the Jews got the upper hand over those who hated them" (Esther 9:10). Culminating in the annual celebration of Purim. And providing a convenient place to take leave of the entries that comprise the Old Testament, in anticipation of what would follow.

Prophecy Fulfilled

QUALIFICATIONS ASIDE, THE INTERIM between the old and new testament has aptly been described as *the silent years*. "It seemed as if God had tired of speaking to those who continued to turn a deaf ear toward him. The school of the prophets has withered an on the vine. While this was a relief for some, it seemed a tragedy for others."[1] As for the latter, "For if you remain silent, I will be like those who have gone down to the pit" (Psa. 28:1)

The silent years were certainly not uneventful. Philip of Macedon initiated the Hellenic League as a rival to Persia. He was succeeded by his youthful son Alexander. Alexander subsequently extended his empire from the Balkans south to Egypt and east to India. Eleven years after his invasion of Asia Minor, he lay dead at the age of thirty-three. Hellenism would survive its militant advocate.

"Hellenism played to mixed reviews. Some saw it as a serious threat to prized religious traditions, their identity as Jews being at stake. Others welcomed Hellenism as a liberating force from ethnic constraints, so much so that their tradition proved an embarrassment."[2] Antiochus IV brought matters to a head. In a dramatic encounter outside Alexandria, a Roman envoy demanded that he cut short his invasion of Egypt. With visions of grandeur shattered and prestige diminished, he bitterly retreated. Along the way, he decided to take out his frustration on Jerusalem, and solidity his southern flank. His mandate promulgating Hellenism and prohibiting Judaism was enforced with utmost severity.

---

1. Inch, *Scripture as Story*, 113.
2. Ibid., 114.

Prophecy Fulfilled

This gave rise to the Maccabean revolt. Increasing numbers of Jews joined in the insurrection. They were eventually able to recover Jerusalem. The altar dedicated to Jupiter was removed and replaced by an alternative devoted to the worship of Yahweh. Subsequently freed from taxation, it was considered tantamount to independence.

The religious idealism of the Maccabees began to decline. When news of the deteriorating conditions reached Rome, Pompey decided to intervene. As expressed by Josephus, Judea was *made tributary to the Romans.*

Herod the Great was the son of the Idumean governor Antipater. He was appointed tetrarch of Judea in 41 BC. His building projects were legion. He zealously protected himself against any usurper. His atrocities are well documented. The state was set for the advent of Jesus as the promised Messiah.

Once when Zechariah's division was serving at the temple, an angel appeared to him. "Do not be afraid, your prayer has been heard," the visitor reassured him. "Your wife Elizabeth will bear you a son, and you are to give him the name John. And he will go on before the Lord, in the spirit and power of Elijah, to turn the hearts of the fathers to their children, and the disobedient to the wisdom of the righteous—to make ready a people prepared for the Lord" (Luke 1:13, 17). Bringing to mind the prophecy of Malachi in this regard (cf. 4:5–6).

God also sent the angel Gabriel to Nazareth, to a virgin pledged to be married. "Greetings, you who are highly favored!" the visitor said to her (Luke 1:28). Mary was understandably troubled by his words, and wondered as to their meaning. "You will be with child and give birth to a son, and you are to give him the name Jesus," Gabriel continued. "He will be great and will be called the Son of the Most High. The Lord God will give him the throne of his father David, and he will reign over the house of Jacob forever; his kingdom will never end."

"I am the Lord's servant, Mary answered. "May it be to me as you have said." As an expression of obedient trust.

Now when John was birthed, Zechariah rejoiced: "And you, my child, will be called a prophet of the Most High; for you will go on before the Lord to prepare the way for him, to give his people the knowledge of salvation through the forgiveness of their sins, because of the tender mercy of our God." The child matured, and became *strong in spirit.* He lived in the wilderness prior to his public ministry. Implying that God was preparing for the demanding task that lay ahead.

The Divine Mandates

In those days Caesar Augustus issued a decree that a census should be taken of the entire Roman world. So Joseph went up from Nazareth to Bethlehem, because he belonged to the line of David. Mary accompanied him, while expecting the birth of her child. While they were there, she gave birth to her firstborn. She wrapped him in cloths, and they placed him in a manger—since there was not room for them in the inn. This was likely an enclosure for the animals, adjacent to the family accommodations.

There were at the time shepherds nearby keeping watch over their flocks at night, when an angel appeared to them. "Today in the town of David a Savior has been born to you," he heartily announced; "he is Christ the Lord" (Luke 2:11)

Suddenly a great company of the heavenly host appeared along with the angel, praising God and saying: "Glory to God in the highest, and on earth peace to men on whom his favor rests." Having delivered their glad tidings, they retreated to their heavenly abode. Leaving the shepherds to see for themselves. After which, they "returned, glorifying and praising God for all the things they had heard and seen, which were just as they had been told."

When the time of their purification was completed, Joseph and Mary took Jesus to Jerusalem to present him to the Lord, and to sacrifice according to the Mosaic instructions. In this instance, indicative of their modest means. There they encountered Simeon, "who was righteous and devout. He was waiting for the consolation of Israel, and the Holy Spirit was upon him." It had been revealed to him that he would not die before seeing the Messiah. Taking Jesus in his arms, he allowed: "Sovereign Lord, as you have promised, you now dismiss your servant in peace. For my eyes have seen your salvation, which you have prepared in the sight of all people, a light for revelation to the Gentiles and for glory to your people Israel."

There was also a prophetess named *Anna*. She was widowed, advanced in years, and worshiped in the temple day and night. "Coming up to them at that very moment, she gave thanks to God and spoke about the child to all who were looking forward to the redemption of Jerusalem." Recalling the sage advice, "Good news should be shared."

When Joseph and Mary had done everything required of them, they returned to Nazareth. "And the child grew and became strong; he was filled with wisdom, and the grace of God was upon him." In every way, setting an enviable example.

Prophecy Fulfilled

When Jesus was twelve years of age, the family went up to Jerusalem to celebrate the Passover. After the festival was over, his parents were returning when they realized that Jesus was not with family or friends. Upon returning to Jerusalem, they discovered him in the temple courts, "sitting among the teachers, listening to them and asking them questions." Persons were amazed at his understanding.

"Son, why have you treated us like this?" his mother inquired. "Your father and I have been anxiously searching for you." She appears perplexed.

"Why were you searching for me?" Jesus asked. "Didn't you know I had to be in my Father's house?" He seems similarly perplexed. "The he went down to Nazareth with them, and was obedient to them." Thus assuring us that it was his intent to honor his parents, and "Jesus grew in wisdom and stature, and in favor with God and men." Thus concludes the brief account of his youth.

Fast forward. John "went into all the country around the Jordan, preaching a baptism of repentance for the forgiveness of sins" (Luke 3:3). Graphically characterized as *the drama of decision*. Jesus also came to be baptized. When John questioned whether this was appropriate, Jesus insisted—apparently as a means of identifying with those he had come to redeem.

Jesus, full of the Holy Spirit, was led by the Spirit into the wilderness. There to be severely tempted by the devil. Whose intent was to compromise his redemptive mission, but without success. After which, the devil departed "until an opportune time" (Luke 4:13). Perhaps when weary from well doing, or experiencing intense opposition.

Jesus then returned to Galilee in the power of the Spirit, news about him spread throughout the countryside. He taught in their synagogues, and received their praise. Incidentally, those thought qualified to teach were supposed to be knowledgeable and able to communicate effectively.

He returned to Nazareth, and went to the synagogue—as was his custom. Handed the Isaiah scroll from which to read, he found the place where it was written: "The Spirit of the Lord is on me, because he has anointed me to preach good news to the poor. He has sent me to proclaim freedom for the prisoners and recovery of sight for the blind, to release the oppressed, to proclaim the year of the Lord's favor" (cf. Isa. 61:1–2). He stopped pointedly short of reference to "the day of vengeance of our God." It was Jubilee imagery applied to the advent of the Messiah.

Jesus then rolled up the scroll and sat down, in anticipation of teaching. "Today this scripture is fulfilled in your hearing," he observed. Those present were initially impressed, and marveled that one raised in their midst could be so gifted. From this point, the situation rapidly deteriorated. With the result that they were determined to do away with him. He, however, walked through their midst, and continued on his way. If this constituted a miracle, it was decidedly not the kind for which they had hoped.

Jesus' public ministry was of relatively brief duration. Initially, the populace was impressed by the fact that he taught with authority (cf. Matt. 7:28–29). As noted above, they applauded his teaching. Until or unless it conflicted with some invested interest. Miracles served to validate his ministry and reflect his compassion.

Jesus gathered disciples around him, and taught them by word and deed. He singled out the apostles to act on his behalf. Recalling the Talmudic observation, "The one sent is as the one who sends." He was both commended and criticized for befriending *sinners*, those who were religiously non-observant. He defended this practice on the grounds that he had come to seek and save that which was lost.

Opposition continued to build. He alerted the Twelve of his impending demise, and subsequent resurrection (cf. Luke 18:31–33). While they did not grasp his meaning at the time, they would recall his words. God works in mysterious ways, which often become increasingly clear with the passing of time. This proved to be no exception.

The passion accounts consist of Jesus' resolve to pursue God's will in the face of adversity and suffering. In this regard, he prayed: "Father, if you are willing, take this cup from me; yet not my will, but yours be done" (Luke 22:42). If it were possible to achieve God's redemptive purpose in some other way, he would welcome the reprieve.

This proved not to be the case. "The men who were guarding Jesus began mocking and beating him. They blindfolded him and demanded, "Prophesy! Who hit you?" And they said many other insulting things to him." Thus adding insult to injury.

When they came to the place called *the Skull*, they crucified him. "Father, forgive them," Jesus petitioned, "for they do not know what they are doing" (Luke 23:34). Thus exhibiting remarkable consideration for others under excruciating conditions. He subsequently cried out, "Father, into your hands I commit my spirit." His trust had triumphed.

Prophecy Fulfilled

The centurion, having witnessed what had transpired, praised God and allowed: "Surely this was a righteous man." Those who were standing by expressed their remorse. Joseph, a member of the Sanhedrin, having not consented to its decision, meant to give Jesus' remains a proper burial. Pilate granted his request.

The perpetrators must have heaved a collective sigh of relief, but their euphoria was short lived. On the first day of the week, women intent on anointing the deceased arrived at the tomb. They found the stone rolled away, and Jesus' body missing. While they were wondering what had happened, two figures in radiant clothing appeared. "Why do you look for the living among the dead?" they inquired. "He is not here, he is risen!" (Luke 24:5–6).

"For what I received I passed on to you as first importance, that Christ died for our sins according to the Scriptures, and that he appeared to Peter, and then to the Twelve." Paul allows. "After that, he appeared to more than five hundred of the brothers at the same time, most of who are still living. Then he appeared to James, and then to all the apostles, and last of all to me also" (1 Cor. 15:3–7). Recalling the liturgical response, "He is risen indeed!"

Jesus initially instructed his disciples to *wait* until endued with power from on high. In greater detail, "But you will receive power when the Holy Spirit comes on you, and you will be my witnesses in Jerusalem, and in all Judea and Samaria, and to the ends of the earth" (Acts 1:8). This should be understood in terms of "cause and effect. Effective witness can only be borne where the Spirit is, and where the Spirit is, effective witness will always follow."[3] Whether by way of guidance, enablement, or favorable response.

Then, too, witness first to those close at hand. As concerned family and friends. Once the pattern is established, reach out to others. Resulting in a succession of witnesses.

"After Jesus said this, he was taken up before their very eyes, and a cloud hid him from their sight." In biblical imagery, this appears to be a symbol of divine glory (cf. Exod. 16:10). No less visible for that reason.

The ascension thus provides an important addition to the gospel narrative. It may be likened to the return of a victorious military leader to the acclaim of the populace. After which, he is able to intercede on behalf of his followers.

---

3. Williams, *Acts*, 24.

Accordingly, "For we do not have a high priest who is unable to sympathize with our weaknesses, but we have one who has been tempted in every way, just as we are—yet without sin. Let us then approach the throne of grace with confidence, so that we may receive mercy and find grace to help us in our time of need" (Heb 4:15–16). More expressly, Jesus promises to dispatch the Holy Spirit (cf. John 15:26).

When the day of Pentecost had come, they were all together in the same lace. As a reminder that the role of discipleship eventuates in community. To experience life together. Available to others, and for their ministry in return.

"Suddenly a sound like the blowing of a violent wind came from heaven and filled the whole house where they were sitting. They saw what seemed to be tongues of fire that separated and came to rest on each of them" (Acts 2:2–3). *Like* and *seemed to be* suggest that his resembled but was not identical to natural occurrences.

"All of them were filled with the Holy Spirit and began to speak in other tongues, as the Spirit enabled them." It is not clear whether all or some spoke in other tongues. The reference could be to ecstatic utterance, an actual language, or a combination of the two. Since some heard them speak in their language. It would seem to rule out the first of these options.

Studies have shown that one may express sounds of a foreign language during times of ecstasy. Although not necessarily knowing its meaning. Which would provide a plausible solution. In any case, this appears to symbolize the reversal of the diffusion of tongues at the Tower of Babel. Thus a coming together for righteous purposes.

So it was that Peter reminded those observing the event that the Lord had promised to pour out his Spirit on *all people*. "With many other words he warned them, and he pleaded with them, "Save yourselves from this corrupt generation." Those who accepted his message were baptized, and about three thousand were added to their number that day." This constituted a remarkable response.

"They devoted themselves to the apostles' teaching and the fellowship, to the breaking of bread and to prayer." "This teaching was authoritative because it was the teaching of the Lord communicated through the apostles in the power of the Spirit. For believers of other generations the New Testament scriptures form the written deposit of the apostolic teaching."[4]

---

4. Bruce, *The Book of the Acts*, 73.

The apostolic fellowship found expression in a number of practical ways, such as *the breaking of bread* and *prayer*. As for the former, this may have included both a common meal and communion. As for the latter, both private and public prayer. "And the Lord added to their number daily those who were being saved."

When approached by a crippled beggar, Peter responded: "Silver or gold I do not have, but what I have I give you. In the name of Jesus Christ of Nazareth, walk" (Acts 3:6). Taking him by his hand, the apostle helped him to his feet. "When all the people saw him walking and praising God, they were filled with wonder and amazement at what had happened to him." Prompting Peter again to share the good news.

Not all were pleased with this turn of events. Peter and John were brought before the Sanhedrin, which ordered them to desist from their labors. "Judge for yourselves whether it is right in God's sight to obey you rather than God," they replied. "For we cannot help speaking about what we have seen and heard" (Acts 4:19-20). After further threatening them, the authorities allowed them to take their leave.

"All the believers were one in heart and mind. No one claimed that any of his possessions was his own, but they shared everything they had." On a voluntary basis, as the need dictated.

As their numbers were increasing, the Grecian Jews complained that their Hebraic counterpart was receiving preferred treatment in the distribution of food. So the Twelve observed: "It would not be right for us to neglect the ministry of the word of God in order to wait on tables. Brothers, choose seven men from among you who are known to be full of the Spirit and wisdom. We will turn this responsibility over to them, and will give our attention to prayer and the ministry of the word" (Acts 6:2-4). This suggestion was met with approval.

Stephen was one of those chosen. When brought before the Sanhedrin to answer to charges brought against him, he gave a spirited defense. "You stiff-necked people!" he exclaimed. "You always resist the Holy Spirit! Was there ever a prophet your fathers did not persecute?" (Acts 7:51-52). When they heard this, they were furious. And when he reported seeing the Son of Man standing at the right hand of God, they dragged him out of the city, and began to stone him. While they were doing so the martyr prayed: "Lord, do not hold this sin against them." And Saul was there, giving approval to his execution.

The Divine Mandates

Saul continued to threaten the disciples. He went to the high priest and asked authorization to bring any of those belonging to the *Way* in Damascus back to Jerusalem. But as he neared his destination, suddenly a light from heaven flashed around him, and he heard a voice saying: "Saul, Saul, why do you persecute me?" (Acts 9:4). It was the voice of Jesus. Consequently, the aggressive persecutor of the Christian fellowship became its zealous advocate.

Our attention is drawn back to Peter. There was at Caesarea a God-fearing Gentile named *Cornelius*, who was approached by an angel. Informed concerning the apostle, he sent a delegation to invite Peter to visit him.

About noon the following day as the delegation was approaching their destination, Peter fell into a trance. In which he saw heaven opened and something resembling a large sheet being let down to earth. It contained all kind of creatures. Then he heard a voice saying, "Get up, Peter. Kill and eat" (Acts 10:13). When protesting that he had never eaten anything unclean, the voice enjoined: Do not call anything impure that God has made clean."

So it was that when the delegation arrived, the apostle agreed to accompany them. As a result, he concluded: I now realize how true it is that God does not show favoritism but accepts men from every nation who fear him and do what is right." While still speaking, the Holy Spirit came on those assembled. Upon learning what had transpired, the believers in Judea "had no further objections and praised God, saying, 'So then, God has granted even the Gentiles repentance unto life'" (Acts 11:18).

Now those who were scattered by the persecution concerning Stephen traveled as far as Phoenicia, Cyprus, and Antioch, sharing the good news with Jews. Some of them, however, began to include Greeks as well. When this was reported to the church at Jerusalem, they sent Barnabas to Antioch to investigate the matter. He was favorably impressed with the results, and went to Tarsus to enlist Saul in the ongoing efforts.

It was about this time when Herod arrested some of the disciples. He put James, the brother of John, to death. When he saw this pleased the Jews, he proceeded to seize Peter as well. So Peter was kept in prison, while the church continued to intercede on his behalf.

Suddenly an angel appeared, urging the apostle accompany him out of the prison. Then, when they had made their escape, the angel left him. Leaving him to make his way to where certain of the disciples were met in prayer. When he could not be found, Herod had the guards executed. The ruler soon joined them in death. "But the word of God continued to increase and spread" (Acts 12:24).

While the leaders of the church at Antioch were worshiping and fasting, the Holy Spirit enjoined them: "Set apart for me Barnabas and Saul for the work to which I have called them" (Acts 13:2). So after they had fasted and prayed, they placed their hands on them and sent them on their way. After considerable success, they returned.

Some men had come down from Jerusalem to Antioch, and were insisting: "Unless you are circumcised, according to the custom taught by Moses, you cannot be saved: (Acts 15:1). Paul (Saul) and Barnabas took issue, and so a delegation was sent to Jerusalem to explore the matter. As a result, the council declared: "It seemed good to the Holy Spirit and to us not to burden you with anything beyond the following requirements: You are to abstain from food sacrificed to idols, from blood, from the meat of strangled animals and from sexual immorality. You will do well to avoid these things." Features reminiscent of God's covenant with Noah.

Now there was a disagreement between Paul and Barnabas, so that they parted ways. Paul chose Silas to accompany him throughout the region of Phrygia and Galatia, having been kept by the Holy Spirit from preaching the word in the province of Asia" (Acts 16:6). Details are lacking.

"When they came to the border of Mysia, they tried to enter Bithynia, but the Spirit of Jesus would not allow them to." Again details are lacking.

"So they passed by Mysia and went down to Troas." Paul had a vision during the night of a man pleading, "Come over to Macedonia and help us." The apostle and his companions assumed that God was calling them to heed the petition.

Their extended itinerary included Philippi, Thessalonica, and Berea, before arriving at Athens. "Although Athens had long since lost the political eminence which was hers in an earlier day, she continued to represent the highest level of culture attained in classical antiquity. The sculpture, literature, and oratory of Athens in the fifth and fourth century B.C. have, indeed, never been surpassed."[5] Along with other noteworthy accomplishments.

It was, however, the pervasive display of idols that caught Paul's attention. He reasoned in the synagogue with Jews and God-fearing Gentiles, and in the marketplace with those who happened to be there. Some inquired, "What is this babbler tying to say?" (Acts. 17:18). While others

---

5. Ibid., 329.

reasoned, "He seems to be advocating foreign gods"—concerning his allusion to Jesus and the resurrection.

There was in Athens a venerable institution, "the Court of the Areopagus, which exercised jurisdiction in matters of religion and morality. Before this body, then, Paul was brought, not to stand trial in a forensic sense, but simply to have an opportunity of expounding his teaching before experts."[6] Having done so, some took issue with his account of the resurrection, favoring instead the Greek notion concerning the immortality of the soul, while others hoped to explore the matter further, and a few embraced the apostle's teaching.

In retrospect, Paul compares himself with certain false prophets: "I have worked much harder, been in prison more frequently, been flogged more severely, and been exposed to death time and again" (2 Cor. 11:23). In his defense before Agrippa, Paul boldly declared: "Short time or long—I pray God that not only you but all who are listening to me today may become what I am, except for these chains: (Acts 29)

Turning to John in closing: "I, John, your brother and companion in the suffering and kingdom and patient endurance that are ours in Jesus, was on the island of Patmos because for the word of God and the testimony of Jesus" (Rev. 1:9). Patmos was a small rocky island in the Aegean Sea, which may have served as a penal colony.

"On the Lord's Day I was in the Spirit," John continues, "and I heard behind me a loud voice like a trumpet, which said, 'Write on a scroll what you see and send it to the seven churches: to Ephesus, Smyrna, Pergamum, Thyatira, Sardis, Philadelphia, and Laodicea."

When John turned around to see who was speaking, he observed someone *like the son of man* standing among seven golden lamp stands—representing the seven churches. Upon seeing this imposing figure, John fell at his feet. "Then he placed his right hand on me and said: "Do not be afraid. I am the First and the Last. I am the Living One' I was dead, and behold I am alive for ever and ever! And I hold the keys of death and Hades." After which, John was enjoined to record that which he had seen, "what is now and what will take place later."

There follows letters to the seven churches. For instance, concerning the church at Ephesus: "I know your deeds, your hard work and your perseverance. Yet I hold this against you. You have forsaken your first love.

---

6. Ibid., 333.

Remember the height from which you have fallen!" (Rev. 2:2, 4–5). Along with an appeal for repentance.

"The great throne room vision of chapters 4 and 5 serves to remind believers living in the shadow of impending persecution that an omnipotent and omniscient God is still in control."[7] Successive visions further explore the precarious role of the Christian community in a cosmic struggle of major proportions.

"He who testifies to these things says, 'Yes, I am coming soon'" (Rev. 22:20). "At the very close of the book is the confession that the answers to the problems of life do not lie in people's ability to create a better world but in the return of the One whose sovereign power controls the course of human affairs. It is for the final act of the great drama of redemption that the church waits with longing."[8]

"Amen. Come, Lord Jesus."

---

7. Mounce, *The Book of Revelation*, 116.
8. Ibid., 410.

Apostolic Fathers

THE DESIGNATION APOSTOLIC FATHERS refers to late first and early second century Christian writers thought to have been personally acquainted with one or more of the apostles. As such, they provide a uniquely valuable commentary on the apostles' teaching. So it is that divine instruction is passed on from one generation to the next, as a cherished legacy.

"The spirit of the Apostolic Fathers was one of preservation, of holding fast to the transmitted truths."[1] This was in keeping with the previously mentioned observation that the early Christian fellowship "devoted themselves to the apostles' teaching" (Acts 2:42). Consequently, as a corporate commitment. In opposition to false teachers, who are alluded to on occasion.

Clement of Rome serves as a prime case in point. Said to be the author of *The Epistle to the Corinthians*, he was the bishop of Rome from 88 to 97 A.D. "A feud had broken out in the Church of Corinth. Presbyters appointed by Apostles, or their immediate successors, had been unlawfully deposed. A spirit of insubordination was rife. The letter of Clement was written to rebuke these irregularities."[2] An allusion to persecution is given by way of explaining the delay in addressing this critical issue.

"Anyone who has stayed with you has experienced the high quality and steadfastness of your faith," Clement allows. "Everyone has marveled at the serious and gentile piety you have displayed in Christ. For in everything

---

1. Musurillo, *The Fathers of the Primitive Church*, 29.
2. Lightfoot, *The Apostolic Fathers*, 11.

you acted without respect of persons, walking in the ways of God, obedient to your superiors and paying due respect to the elders among you."[3]

After an opening accolade of praise, Clement touches on the roots of their trouble: jealousy and envy. Which have a long history in the Old Testament narratives, and played a critical role in the death of the martyrs. Whether present in the community or the fellowship itself.

"Clement, then, wanted to remind the Corinthians of the noble truths of the faith into which they had been baptized, and to underline the importance of humility and obedience in Christianity."[4] In this regard, "we are writing this to you as a reminder to ourselves as much as an admonition to you; for we too are in the same arena, facing the same sort of contest. Hence let us do away with all silly, foolish preoccupations and come to that which is the glorious and venerable norm of our teaching, and see what is good, pleasant and acceptable in the sight of Him who made us" (7).

"For Christ is with them that are lowly of mind, not with them that exalt themselves over the flock. The scepter of God, even our Lord Jesus Christ, came not in the pomp of arrogance or of pride, though he might have done so, but in lowliness of mind" (16). In keeping with the motif of the Suffering Servant (cf. Isa. 53).

"Let us be imitators also of them which went about in goatskins and sheepskins, preaching the Coming of Christ. We mean Elijah and Elisha and likewise Ezekiel, the prophets, and besides them those men also that obtained a good report." (17). As with Abraham, who was called the friend of God. As with Job, who refrained from evil. As with Moses, who remained faithful. As with David, who earnestly repented of the evil he had done.

"Seeing then that we have been partakers of many great and glorious doings, let us hasten to return unto the goal of peace which hath been handed down to us from the beginning, and let us look steadfastly unto the Father and Maker of the whole world, and cleave unto His splendid and excellent gifts of peace and benefits," Clement exhorts his readers. Let us behold him in our mind, and let us look with the eyes of our soul unto His longsuffering will" (19).

Do not hesitate, as if uncertain of the course set by the apostles. Nor fearful of the repercussions. In confidence of God's sustaining grace. With cognizance of the goals set before us. In anticipation of God's lavish blessings.

3. *The Epistle of Clement to the Corinthians*, 1.
4. Lightfoot, *The Apostolic Fathers*, 52.

The Divine Mandates

"Let us therefore approach Him in holiness of soul, lifting up pure and undefiled hands unto Him, with love towards our gentle and compassionate Father who made us an elect portion unto Himself" (29). As a people cleansed and set apart for God's purposes. Without reproach and by way of righteous example.

"Seeing then that we are the special portion of a Holy God, let us do all things that pertain unto holiness, forsaking evil-speaking, abominable and impure embraces, drunkenness and tumults and hateful lusts, abominable adultery, hateful pride" (30). Thus cultivating a life free from inconsistency and ambiguity.

"In Sections 37 to 38 Clement compares the Church to an army, in which not everyone can be prefects, tribunes, or centurions; but, just as in an army, all must be obedient to the commands of the generals. The Church is also like a body, and the head cannot operate without the smallest members."[5] Like a mighty army, united in a common cause. Disciplined and devoted.

In greater detail, "Let not the strong neglect the weak; and let the weak respect the strong. Let the rich minister too the poor; and let the poor give thanks to God, because He has given him one through whom his wants may be supplied. Let the wise display his wisdom, not in words, but in good works" (38). Moreover, since we derive all things from God, let us render thanks for all things to him.

"Senseless and stupid and foolish and ignorant men jeer and mock at us, desiring that they themselves should be exalted in their imagination. For what power has a mortal or what strength has a child of earth?" (39). Instead, one is accountable to God, who dispenses justice without exception. Regarding both those demeaned and those demeaning others.

Clement likewise reminds his readers that things should be done decently and in order. Not in a haphazard fashion, according to the whims of the participants. Nor to further some partisan interest, without consideration for the welfare of all concerned.

"The Apostles received the Gospel for us from the Lord Jesus Christ; Jesus Christ was sent forth from God. So then Christ is from God, and the apostles are from Christ. Both therefore come from the will of God in the appointed order" (41). In the order appointed by God: concerning Christ, the apostles, and meant to be preserved for subsequent generations. As set over against those who take issue or waver in their determination.

---

5. Musurillo, *The Fathers of the Primitive Search*, 54.

In greater detail, the apostles "having received a charge, and (being) fully assured through the resurrection of our Lord Jesus Christ and confirmed in the word that the kingdom of God had come. (So) they appointed their first-fruits, when they had proved them by the Spirit, to be bishops and deacons."

"And our Apostles knew through our Lord Jesus Christ that there would be strife over the name of the bishop's office. For this cause therefore, having perceived complete foreknowledge, to appoint the aforesaid persons, and afterwards they provided a continuance, that if these should fall asleep, other approved men should succeed in their ministration" (44). Conversely, "For we see that you have displaced certain persons, though they were living honorably, from the ministration which had been respected by them blamelessly." Thus in contradiction to the apostolic intent. What is to be done? "Be contentious, brethren, and jealous about the things that pertain unto salvation. You have searched the scriptures, which are true, which are given through the Holy Ghost; and you know that nothing unrighteous or counterfeit is written in them. You will not find that righteous persons have been thrust out by holy men" (45). Righteous people were persecuted, while ignoring the *lawless*.

"Wherefore are there strifes and wraths and factions and divisions and war among you? Have we not one God and one Christ and one Spirit of grace that was shed upon us? And is there not one calling in Christ?" Clement rhetorically inquires. "Your division has perverted many; it has brought many to despair, many to doubting, and all of us to sorrow. And your sedition still continues" (46).

Remember the apostle Paul's ministry among you, and be encouraged to do the right thing. It is shameful, dearly beloved, yes, utterly shameful and unworthy of your conduct in Christ, that it should be reported that the very steadfast and ancient Church of the Corinthians, for the sake of one or two persons, makes sedition against its presbyters," Clement protests. "And this report has reached not only us, but them also which differs from us, so that you even heap blasphemies on the Name of the Lord by reason of your folly, and moreover create peril for yourselves" (47). Thus losing out all around.

"Let us therefore root this out quickly, and let us fall down before the Master and entreat Him with tears, that He may show Himself propitious and be reconciled unto us, and may restore us to the seemly and pure conduct which belongs to our love of the brethren" (48). Consequently, portraying the problem from the perspective of the apostolic community, rather than some partisan derivative.

"Let him that has love in Christ fulfil the commandment of Christ. Love joins us unto God; love endures a multitude of sins; love endures all things, is long-suffering in all things. There is nothing arrogant in love. Love has no divisions, love makes no sedition, love does all things in accord" (49). The elect are made perfect in love, and lacking love, God is displeased.

"For all our transgressions which we have committed through any of the wiles of the adversary, let us entreat that we may obtain forgiveness. Yes and they also, who set themselves up as leaders of faction and division, ought to look to the common ground of hope For it is good for a man to make confession of his trespasses rather than to burden his heart" (51). Whether in regard to the problem addressed, or some other.

"For you know, and know well, the sacred scriptures, dearly beloved, and you have searched into the oracles of God. We write these things therefore to put you in remembrance" (53). *In remembrance* of both Old and New Testament writings, but most notably the latter. Not something with which they were unfamiliar, but to recall the foundation on which their faith was built.

"Who therefore is noble among you? Who is compassionate? Who is fulfilled with love? Let him say, if by reason of me there be faction and strife and divisions, I retire, I depart, whither you will, and I do that which is ordered by the people: only let the flock of Christ be at peace with its duly appointed presbyters" (54). As a worse case scenario, should reconciliation seem beyond reach. "He that shall have done this, shall win for himself great renown in Christ, and every place will receive him."

"Therefore let us also make intercession for them that are in any transgression, that forbearance and humility may be given them, to the end that they may yield not unto us, but unto the will of God" (56). Not to prove a point, but to achieve a goal. Resulting in corporate blessing.

If not leave, then learn. "You therefore that laid the foundation of the sedition, submit yourselves unto the presbyters and receive chastisement unto repentance, bending the knees of your heart. Learn to submit yourselves, laying aside the arrogant and proud stubbornness of your tongue" (57).

"Receive our counsel, and you shall have no occasion of regret" (58). "But if certain persons should be disobedient unto the words spoken by Him through us, let them understand that they will entangle themselves in no slight transgression and danger" (59). For much is at stake, concerning those who have created the problem, and the fellowship as a whole.

Having pled with those at fault, Clement then petitions "that we may set our hope on Your Name which is the primal source of all creation, and open the eyes of our hearts, that we may know You, who alone abides Highest in the lofty, holy in the holy; who sets the lowly on high, and brings the lofty low. We beseech you, Lord and Master to be our help and succor" (59). For much is at stake, concerning those who have created the problem, and the fellowship as a whole.

Having pled with those at fault, Clement then petitions "that we may set our hope on Your Name with is the primal source of all creation, and open the eyes of our hearts, that we may know You, who alone abides Highest in the lofty, holy in the holy; who sets the lowly on high, and brings the lofty low. We beseech You, Lord and Master to be our help and succor" (59). Recalling the poignant text, "Unless the Lord builds the house, its builders labor in vain" (Psa. 127:1)

"You, Lord, created the earth," Clement heartily acknowledges. "You are faithful throughout all generations, righteous in Your judgments, marvelous in strength and excellence. You are wise in creating and prudent in establishing that which You have made. Lay not to our account every sin of Your servants and Your handmaids, but cleanse us with the cleansing of Your truth" (60). As a means of living in God's world, by means of amazing grace.

Grant to those in authority "O Lord, health, peace, concord, stability, that they may administer the government which you have given them without failure. O Lord, direct their counsel according to that which is good and well-pleasing in Your sight, that, administering in peace and gentleness with godliness the power which You have given them, they may obtain Your favor" (61). Consequently, reflecting a wisdom from above.

With the conclusion of his prayer, Clement summarizes as his purpose for writing: "to touch on 'every topic of faith and repentance and authentic love,' reminding them of their obligation to live in harmony. They are men who have kept the faith and have scrutinized the sayings of God's revelation. Hence they must cease from conflict, and for this Clement has sent aged and prudent men to be 'delegates between you and us.'"[6] In his role as a highly esteemed member of the apostolic fathers.

---

6. Ibid., 56.

The Divine Mandates

More explicit in its intent is the *Didarche* or *The Teaching of the Apostles*. Thought to be a second century church manual, it consists of a moral treatise and instructions for ecclesiastical procedure. In language and subject matter, it reveals a close affinity to other early documents of the emerging church.

"There are two ways one of life and one of death, and there is a great difference between the two ways. The way of life is this. First of all you shall love the God that made you; secondly, your neighbor as yourselves. And all things whatever then you would not have befall yourself, neither do unto another."[7]

The *context* appears derived from the two ways explored in the initial psalm. In greater detail, "Blessed is the man who does not walk in the counsel of the wicked or stand in the way of sinners or sit in the seat of mockers" (v. 1). The terms *walk, stand,* and *sit* are progressive; implying increased deviation from God's gracious design.

Instead, "his delight is in the law of the Lord, and on his law he meditates day and night." He resembles a tree planted by streams of water, which yield its fruit in season and whose leaf does not wither. Hence, resistant to drought and productive.

"Not so the wicked!" Who more resemble the chaff which the wind drives away. Consequently, rootless, without substance, and easily swayed. "For the Lord watches over the way of the righteous, but the way of the wicked will perish."

However, its *content* has drawn Jesus' instruction, as preserved by the apostolic circle. "Teacher, which is the greatest commandment in the Law?" *an expert in the law* inquired of him.

"'Love the Lord your God with all your heart and with all your soul and with all your mind.'" He replied. "This is the first and greatest commandment. And the second is like it, 'Love your neighbor as yourself.' All the Law and the Prophets hang on these two commandments" (Matt. 22:36–40). *Love* as here expressed involves commitment. In other words, love is as love does.

In addition, the love of God and others are bonded together. "If anyone says, 'I love Good,' yet hates his brother, he is a liar. For anyone who does not love his brother, whom he has seen, cannot love God, whom he has not seen. And he has given us this command: Whoever loves God must also love his brother'" (1 John 4:20–21).

---

7. *Didarche*, 1.

Coupled with the above teaching, Jesus enjoined his disciples: "Do to others as you would have them do to you" (Luke 6:31). "Now of these words the doctrine is this. Bless them that curse you, and pray for your enemies and fast for them that persecute you; for what thanks is it if you love them that love you? Do not the Gentiles do the same: But love them that hate you, and you shall not have an enemy" (1). Recalling the admonition, "Do not be overcome by evil, but overcome evil with good" (Rom 12:21).

Give generously from God's rich bounty. Receive only as it is necessary. Do not expect others to do for you what you are unwilling to do for yourselves, as implied while not explicit.

"And this is the second commandment of the teaching," the text continues. "You shall not murder, you shall not commit adultery, you shall not corrupt boys, you shall not commit fornication, you shall not steal, you shall not deal in magic, you shall do no sorcery, you shall not murder a child by abortion nor kill them when born, you shall not covet your neighbor's goods," and so on (2).

All such behavior is in violation of the apostle's teaching. Accordingly, it is unacceptable to the Lord. Whether in keeping with cultural standards or not. As apt commentary, Christians "pass their days on earth, but they are citizens of heaven. They obey the prescribed laws, and at the same time, they surpass the laws by their lives. They love all men, and are persecuted by all."[8]

"My child, flee from every evil and everything that resembles it. Be not angry, for anger leads to murder, nor jealous nor contentious and wrathful; for of all these things murders are engendered." (3) Giving rise to the Jewish notion of building a fence, lest one be tempted to do evil. Recalling a time when a rabbi inquired of me, "What is wrong with building fences?" When I deferred to him, he replied: "Nothing is wrong with building fences if we do not worship them." Thus falling prey to legalism and idolatry.

"You have heard that it was said to the people long ago, 'Do not murder, and anyone who murders will be subject to judgment,'" Jesus observed. "But I tell you that anyone who is angry with his brother will be subject to judgment" (Matt. 5:21–22). While murder is not explicit in anger, it is implicit.

"My child, be not lustful, for lust leads to fornication, neither foul-speaking. My child, be no dealer in omen, since it leads to idolatry, nor an enchanter nor an astrologer nor a magician. My child, be not a liar, since

---

8. *The Epistle to Diognetus*, V.

lying leads to theft, neither avaricious neither vainglorious. My child, be not a murmurer, since it leads to blasphemy." In that one reaps what he or she sows.

Instead, "be meek, since the meek shall inherit the earth." Receive as good what occurs, "knowing that nothing is done without God." In this regard, "And we know that in all things God works for the good of those who love him, who have been called according to his purpose" (Rom. 8:28). Not that all things are desirable in and of themselves, but can be a means for working good.

"My child, you shall remember him that speaks to you the word of God," and honor him. Moreover, "you shall seek out the saints, that you may find rest in their words. You shall not make a schism, but you shall pacify those what contend; you shall judge righteously," and so on (4). In these and other ways, to be a catalyst for community.

"You shall hate all hypocrisy, and everything that is not pleasing to the Lord. You shall never forsake the commandment of the Lord; but shall keep those things which you have received, neither adding to them nor taking away from them." Thus compromising the apostolic teaching. "In church you shall confess your transgressions, and shall not engage in prayer with an evil conscience. This is the way of life.

"But the way of death is this. First of all, it is evil and full of a curse" (5). As pertains to murders, adulteries, lusts, thefts, and the like. "May you be delivered, my children, from all these things."

"See lest any man lead you astray from this way of righteousness, for he teaches you apart from God. For if you are able to bear the whole yoke of the Lord, you shall be perfect; but if you are not able, do that which you are able." In this and elsewhere, strive for excellence, and when falling short, one has still accomplished much.

"But concerning eating, bear that which you are able; yet abstain by all means from meat sacrificed to idols; for it is the worship of dead gods." Which allows for conscientious differences, while prohibiting idolatrous worship.

Here the text turns from an exposition of the two ways, to consider ecclesiastical matters. "Having first recited all these things, baptize in the name of the Father and of the Son and of the Holy spirit in living (running) water" (7). But if running water is not available, then otherwise. "But if you have neither, then pour water on the head thrice in the name of the Father and the Son and of the Holy Spirit." But before baptism, let both he who performs it and the one who receives it fast. As for the latter, let it be for a day or two in duration.

And do not fast as the hypocrites, who approach it in a more token fashion. Neither pray as the hypocrites. "And when you pray, do not be like the hypocrites for they love to pray standing in the synagogues and on the street corners to be seen by men," Jesus cautioned. "I tell you the truth, they have received their reward in full" (Matt. 6:5).

Pray rather as the Lord commanded, "Our Father in heaven, hallowed be your name, your kingdom come, your will be done on earth as it is in heaven. Give us today our daily bread. Forgive us our debts, as we also have forgiven our debtors. And lead us not into temptation, but deliver us from the evil one" (Matt. 6:9–13). "Three times a day pray you so" (8).

There follows a series of thanksgivings thought appropriate for communion. This concludes with a conditional invitation, "If any man is holy, let him come; if any man is not let him repent" (1).

"Whosoever therefore shall come and teach you all these things that have been said before, receive him; but if the teacher himself be perverted and teach a different doctrine to the destruction thereof, hear him not" (11). That which is in accord with the apostolic teaching, but nothing that deviates from it.

"But let everyone that comes in the name of the Lord be received; and then when you have tested him you shall know him" (12). That is, do not be quick to judge. Things are not necessarily as they at first appear.

"If he comes as a traveler, assist him, so far as you are able; but he shall not stay with you more than two or three days, if it is necessary. But if he wishes to settle with you, being a craftsman, let him work for his bread. But if he has no craft, according to your wisdom provide how he shall live as a Christian among you, but not in idleness." Initially, "She who emulates Sarah is not ashamed of that highest of ministries, helping wayfarers,"[9] However, hospitality comes with conditions. For one, the stay is to be of a brief period of time. For another, if a craftsman, he is expected to work at his trade. If not, then available for an alternative means of support. As exemplified by the apostle Paul upon arrival in Corinth. "There he met a Jew named Aquila a native of Pontus, who had recently come from Italy with his wife Priscilla. Paul went to see them, and because he was a tentmaker as they were, he stayed and worked with them" (Acts 18:2–3).

---

9. Clement of Alexandria, *The Instructor*, III, x.

The Divine Mandates

"But every true prophet desiring to settle among you is worthy of his food. In like manner a true teacher is also worthy, like the workman, of his food" (13). Drawing upon Jesus' instruction to the seventy-two he sent forth to prepare the way for his arrival (cf. Luke 7:10). Otherwise, give to the poor.

"And on the Lord's own day gather yourselves together and break bread and give thanks, first confessing your transgressions, that your sacrifice may be pure" (14). On the first day of the week, and thus celebrating Jesus' resurrection. And in anticipation of his return. While rejoicing in the good news, readily shared with others.

But only after having confessed one's transgression. Having done that which he or she should not have done, and having left undone that which ought to have been undertaken. Not uncommonly embracing the lesser good, rather than blatant evil, as over against the greater good.

Resulting in sanctified worship. Enlisting a corporate response. One enthusiastically offered. While attentive to divine instruction.

"And let no man, having his dispute with his fellow, join your assembly until they have been reconciled, that your sacrifice may not be defiled." Recalling again Jesus' teaching, as passed on by way of the apostles and their associates. Accordingly, "if you are offering your gift at the altar and there remember that your brother has something against you, leave your gift there in front of the altar. First go and be reconciled to your brother; then come and offer your gift:" (Matt. 5:23–24).

All things considered, in every place and at every time offer the Lord a pure sacrifice. One for which he is adamantly deserving. As a remarkable privilege, of which persons are not deserving.

"Appoint for yourselves therefore bishops and deacons worthy of the Lord, men who are meek and not lovers of money, and true and approved; for unto you they also perform the service of the prophets and teachers. Therefore despise them not; for they are your honorable men along with the prophets and teachers" (15). Thus the congregation is to assume corporate responsibility for delegating authority. Which requires wisdom and discernment, along with a sensitivity to the leading of the Spirit.

Once installed, cooperate to the best of one's ability. Neither expect too much nor too little from them. Be attentive to their leading. Do not denigrate them. If thought necessary, remove them from office—while ministering to their needs. As implied by the thrust of the text.

"And reprove one another, not in anger but in peace, as you find in the Gospel; and let no one speak to any that has gone wrong towards his neighbor, neither let him hear a word from you, until he repent. But your prayers and your almsgiving and all your deeds so do as you find it in the Gospel of our Lord." Yes, *reprove one another.* Rather than ignore situations that should be addressed.

Not with a better-than-thou attitude, calculated to compound the problem. But as one who is also at fault, and desiring of forgiveness. Then also attentive to the reproof of others, whether presently or on some future occasion.

"Be watchful for your life; let your lamps not be quenched and your loins not ungirded, but be ready; for you know not the hour in which our Lord comes. And you shall gather yourselves together frequently, seeking what is fitting for your souls" (16). Thus echoing the appeal, "Let us not give up meeting together, as some are in the habit of doing, but let us encourage one another—and all the more as you see the Day approaching" (Heb 10:25).

"For in the last days the false prophets and corrupters shall be multiplied. And the world deceiver will appear. Then shall the world see the Lord coming upon the clouds of heaven." As attested by the apostles.

The Apologist

THE APOLOGIST ATTEMPTS TO give a reasoned advocacy for his or her faith. This is in keeping with the admonition, "Do your best to present yourself to God as one approved, a workman who does not need to be ashamed and who correctly handles the word of truth." Conversely, "Avoid godless chatter, because those who indulge in it will become more and more ungodly" (2 Tim. 2:15–16).

"Beginning in the second century, a number of Christians addressed defenses of Christianity to the emperor or to the educated public generally, arguing the Christians should not be persecuted, and refuting charges made against them" For instance, "In a world where most people worshiped all sorts of deities, the Christian refusal to do so led to the charge that they were atheists, and the apologists had to explain how this was not so. More fundamentally, most educated Greeks and Romans thought of Christianity as a lower-lass superstition from an obscure frontier province."[1] Inciting the apologists to represent it as intellectually respectable.

"One Christian apologist, Justin Martyr, who came from Palestine (Samaria), settled in Rome, and was killed under persecution about 165, presented Christianity as the best of philosophies. He told how he had studied with different philosophers without finding satisfaction, until one day a mysterious old man taught him about Christian faith."[2] Thus the stage is set for Justin's initial apologetic.

He addresses his correspondence to the Emperor, certain select individuals, and the Senate, along with "the whole People of the Romans, in

---

1. Placher, *A History of Christian Theology*, 59.
2. Ibid.

behalf of those of all nations who are unjustly hated and wantonly abused, myself being one of them"[3] Allowing for the pervasive character of Christian persecution, drawing from a general misunderstanding. Constituting a situation of grave significance for all involved.

"Reason directs those who are truly pious and philosophical to honor and love only what is true, declining to follow traditional opinions, if these be worthless. For not only does sound reason direct us to refuse the guidance of those who did or taught anything wrong, but it is incumbent on the lover of truth, by all means, and if death be threatened to do and say what is right" (2). Consequently, appealing for a common ground, from which his appeal might be launched.

"But lest anyone think that this is an unreasonable and reckless utterance, we demand that the charges against the Christians be investigated, and that, if these be substantiated, they be punished as they deserve. But if no one can convict us of anything, true wisdom forbids you, for the sake of a wicked rumor, to wrong blameless men" (3). Recalling Paul's apt contrast between *the word of truth* and *godless chatter.*

Why are Christians persecuted? Sometimes simply because of the negative implications associated with the name. However, "By the mere application of a name, nothing is decided, either good or evil, apart from the actions implied in the name; and indeed so far at least as one may judge from the name we are accused of, we are most excellent people" (4). Thus coupling the term *Christian* with *excellence.*

As noted above, Christians are also charged with atheism. "And we confess that we are atheists," Justin candidly allows, "so far as gods of this sort are concerned, but not with respect to the most true God, the Father of righteousness and temperance and the other virtues, who is free from all impurity. For both Him, and the Son, and the prophetic Spirit, we worship and adore" (6).

As for the latter, "For, impelled by the desire of the eternal and pure life, we seek the abode that is with God, the Father and Creator of all, and hasten to confess our faith" (8). As worthy of consideration by others, and the welfare of all involved.

As for the former, "And neither do we honor with many sacrifices and garlands of flowers such deities as men have formed and set in shrines and called gods; since we see that these are soulless and dead, and have not the form of God, but have names and forms of those wicked demons which

---

3. Martyr, *The First Apology*, 1.

have appeared. What infatuation!" (9). Such pretense! Quite lacking in credibility.

How is God to be served? "But we have received by tradition that God does not need the material offerings which men can give, see, indeed, that He Himself is the provider of all things. And we have been taught, and are convinced, and do believe, that He accepts those only who imitate the excellences which reside in Him" (10). Recalling the contrary opinion that humans were created to relieve the deities from burdensome duties.

"And when you hear that we look for a kingdom, you suppose, without making any inquiry, that we speak of a human kingdom; whereas we speak of that which is with God, as appears also from the confession of their faith made by those who are charged with being Christians, though they know that death is the punishment award to him who so confesses" (11). But were the kingdom of the world, Christians would not be inclined to embrace martyrdom.

"What sober-minded men, then, will not acknowledge that we are not atheists, worshiping as we do the Maker of this universe" (13). "Our teacher of these things is Jesus Christ, who also was born for this purpose, and was crucified under Pontius Pilate, procurator of Judea, in the times of Tiberius Caesar; and that we reasonably worship Him, having learned that He is the Son of the true God." Consequently, he appeals to a reasoning faith.

"For we forewarned you to be on your guard, lest those demons whom we have been accusing should deceive you, and quite divert you from reading and understanding what we say. For they strive to hold you their slaves and servants; and sometimes by appearances in dreams, and sometimes by magical impositions" (14). Calling for awareness and discretion.

"And everywhere we, more readily than all men, endeavor to pay to those appointed by you the taxes both ordinary and extraordinary, as we have been taught by Him. Whence to God alone we render worship, but in other things we gladly serve you, and praying that with your kingly power you be found to possess also sound judgment" (17). As exemplary citizens, cultivated by the Christian faith.

As for immortality, many are agreed. For instance, "Empedocles and Pythagoras, Plato and Socrates, and the pit of Homer and the descent of Ulysses to inspect these things, and all that has uttered of like kind. Such favor as you grant to these, grant also to us, who not less but more firmly than they believe in God; since we expect to receive again our own bodies, for we maintain that with God nothing is impossible" (18).

The Apologist

"And to the thoughtful person would anything appear more incredible, than, if we were not in the body, and some one were to say that it was possible that from a small drop of human seed bones and sinews and flesh be formed into the shape such as we see. In the same way, then, you are now incredulous because you have never seen a dead man rise again" (19).

Nor that immortality of the soul and the resurrection of life are identical. "Belief in the immortality of the soul is not belief in a revolutionary event. Immortality, in fact, is only a *negative* assertion: the soul does not die, but simply lives on. Resurrection is a *positive* assertion: the whole man, who has really died, is recalled to life by a new act of creation by God."[4] As attested to by the resurrection of Jesus.

There being a proliferation of heathen analogies. As an example, "And the philosophers called Stoics teach that even God Himself shall be resolved into fire., and they say that the world is to be formed anew by this revolution; but we understand that God, the Creator of all things, is superior to the things that are to be changed" (20). Such analogies extend to deferring to Jesus and the *Word* and *Son of God*.

"And that this may now become evident to you—(firstly) that whatever we assert in conformity with what has been taught us by Christ, and by the prophets who preceded Him, are alone true, and are older than all the writers who have existed" (23). Secondly, "that Jesus Christ is the only proper Son who has been begotten by God, becoming man according to His will, He taught us these things for the conversion and restoration of the human race." Thirdly, "before he became man among men, some, influenced by the demons before mentioned," related fictitious accounts concerning what would transpire.

In contrast to common practice, "we have been taught that to expose newly-born children is the part of wicked men; and this we have been taught lest we should do any one an injury, and lest we should sin against God" (27). Such are for the most part employed for prostitution. Not only the girls, but the boys as well. "Indeed, the things which you do openly and with applause, as if the divine light were overturned and extinguished, these you lay to our charge; which, in truth, does no harm to us who shrink from doing any such things, but only to those who bear false witness against us."

"But whether we marry, it is only that we may bring up children," rather than abuse them (29). Or if refraining from marriage, then content with our continence. In

---

4. Cullmann, "Immortality of the Soul or Resurrection of the Dead," 19.

This regard, Paul allows: "for I have learned to be content in any and every situation, whether well fed or hungry, whether living in plenty or in want" (Phil. 4:12).

"There were, then, among the Jews certain men who were prophets of God, through whom the prophetic Spirit published beforehand things that were to come to pass" (31). As concerning the manner in which Christ would be born, as to the place of his birth, and many other regards. "But when you hear the utterances of the prophets spoken as it were personally, you must not suppose that they are spoken by the inspired themselves, but by the Divine Word who moves them" (36).

But lest some suppose that we maintain that things are determined beforehand, "We have learned from the prophets, and we hold it to be true, that punishments, and chastisements, and good rewards, are rendered according to the merit of each man's actions. And again, unless the human race have the power of avoiding evil and choosing good by free choice, they are not accountable for their actions" (43).

Now lest it be understood that we are condemning all who lived before the birth of Christ, "He is the Word of whom every race of men were partakers; and those who lived reasonably are Christians, even though they have been thought atheists; as, among the Greeks, Socrates and Heraclitus" (46). Accordingly, Paul reasoned: "From one man he made every nation of men, that they should inhabit the whole earth; and he determined the times set for them the exact places where they should live. God did this so that men would seek him and perhaps reach out for him and find him, though he is not far from each one of us" (Acts 17:26–27).

"Therefore since we are God's offspring, we should not think that the divine being is like gold or silver or stone—an image made by man's design and skill," the apostle continues. "In the past God overlooked such ignorance, but now he commands all people everywhere to repent. For he has set a day when he will judge the world with justice by the man he has appointed. He has given proof of this to all men by raising him from the dead." In similar manner, Justin concludes: "And we, since the proof of this subject is less needful now, will pass for the present to the proof of those things which are urgent."

As concerns Christ, "I revealed myself to those who did not ask for me; I was found by those who did not seek me. To a nation that did not call on my name. I said, 'Here am I, here am I'" (Isa. 65:1) Conversely, "All day long I have held out my hands to an obstinate people, who walk in ways not good, pursuing their own imaginations—a people who continually provoke me."

Inciting Justin to observe: "For the Jews having the prophecies, and being always in expectation of the Christ to come, did not recognize Him; and not only so, but even treated Him shamefully. But the Gentiles, who had never heard anything about Christ, until the apostles set out from Jerusalem and preached concerning Him, were filled with joy and faith." So the people were alerted, and so it came to pass.

As pertains to Christ's humiliation, "But that, having become man for our sakes, He endured to suffer and to be dishonored. He was wounded for our transgressions, He was bruised for our iniquities, the chastisement of peace was upon him, by his stripes we are healed." (50, cf. Isa. 53:4).

As pertains to his exaltation, Paul allows: "therefore God exalted him in the highest place and gave him the name that is above every name, that at the name of Jesus every knee should bow, in heaven and on earth and under the earth, and every tongue confess that Jesus Christ is Lord, to the glory of God the Father" (Phil. 2:9–11). Which Justin alludes to in a less direct manner.

"Though we cold bring forward many other prophesies, we forbear, judging these sufficient for the persuasion of those who have ears to hear and understand; and considering also that those persons are able to see that we do not make mere assertions without being able to produce proof, like those fables that are told of the so-called sons of Jupiter" (53). "So many things therefore, as these, when they are seen with the eye, are enough to produce conviction and belief in those who embrace the truth, and are not bigoted in their opinions, nor are governed by their passions."

"But in no instance, not even in any of those called sons of Jupiter, did they imitate being crucified; for it was not understood by them, all the things said of it having been put symbolically. And this, as the prophet foretold, is the greatest symbol of His power and rule; as is also proved by the things which fall under our observation" (55). As with the sea, with the sail of a boat lifted overhead. Or with the human body, with arms outstretched.

Not only did the demons attempt to deceive persons before the advent of Jesus as the Messiah, but subsequently as well. So that their resolve remains undiminished. "Wherefore we pray that the sacred senate and your people may, along with yourselves, be arbiters of this our memorial, in order that if any one be entangled by that man's (the Samaritan Simon) doctrines, he may learn the truth, and so be able to escape error; now as for the statue, if you please, destroy it" (56).

"Nor can the devils persuade men that there will be conflagration for the punishment of the wicked; as they were unable to effect that Christ should be hidden after He came" (57). Since both alike are manifest. The former in that persons are inclined to reap what they sow. The latter in that Jesus arose from obscurity, and was subsequently raised from the dead. As seemingly implied by Justin's line of reasoning.

"But only can they effect, that they who irrationally, and were brought up licentiously in wicked customs, and are prejudiced in their own opinions, should kill and hate us; whom we not only do not hate, but, as is proved, pity and endeavor to lead to repentance." Such who fail to recognize that the Christian is taught to return good for evil, as an excuse to retain their evil lifestyle.

As previously mentioned, the demons sponsor Marcion—who advocates a false deity. "And this man many have believed, as if he alone knew the truth, and laugh at us, though they have no proof of what they say, but are carried away irrationally as lambs by a wolf" (58). Being convinced of that which is incredible, while failing to lay hold of that truth made manifest to us.

As a pertinent aside, Justin's line of thought recalls the clinical psychologist Don Tweedie. It sounded to him that persons of faith were asked to abort their reasoning capabilities. Conversely, it seemed to him that if there were a God, who gave persona a mental capacity, one would expect them to employ it. So things continued until he attended a lecture by the erudite Edward John Carnell. Thus convinced that of the prospect of a reasoning faith, he became a devoted disciple.

Justin then speculates that Plato derived from the prophets the observation "that God, having altered matter which was shapeless, made the world" (59). In particular, he singles out Moses as the first prophet, "and of greater antiquity than the Greek writers; and through whom the Spirit of prophesy" was active. By way of implication, those who relish their Greek tradition ought to be more, rather than less, attentive to the teaching of the prophets.

Having alluded to the prophets, Justin turns his attention to the apostles. "And for this (the ordinance of baptism) we have learned from the apostles this reason. Since at our birth we were without our own knowledge or choice, by our parents coming together, and were brought up in bad habits and wicked training; in order that we may not remain the children of necessity and of ignorance, but may become the children of choice and knowledge" (61). Having exercised discernment, then repentance and faith.

After which, Christians assemble together. Having prayed, we greet one another. "There is then brought to the president of the brethren bread, a cup of wine mixed with water; and he taking them, gives praise and glory to the Father of the universe, through the name of the Son and of the Holy Ghost, and offers thanks at considerable length for our being counted worthy to receive these things at His hands" (65).

"And when the president has given thanks, and all the people have expressed their assent (by saying *Amen*). Those who are called by us deacons give to each of those present to partake of the bread and wine mixed with water over which the thanksgiving was pronounced, and to those who are absent they carry away a portion." Which serves not only to explain the practice, but correct the false impression that Christians feasted on human flesh.

"And we afterwards continually remind each other of these things. And the wealthy among us help the needy; and we always keep together; and for all things wherewith we are supplied, we bless the Maker of all through His Son Jesus Christ, and through the Holy Ghost" (67). In greater detail, "And on the day called Sunday, all who live in cities or in the country gather together in one place, and the memoirs of the apostles or the writings of the prophets are read, as long as time permits." When the reader has ceased, "the president verbally instructs, and exhorts to the imitation of these good things." After which, all rise together and pray.

Then throughout the week, Christians are bonded together in service, to one another and others in need. "But Sunday is the day on which we all hold our common assembly, because it is the first day on which God, having wrought a change in the darkness and matter, made the world; and Jesus Christ our Savior on the same day rose from the dead." Having appeared to his disciples, Jesus "taught them these things, which we had submitted to you also for your consideration."

"And if these things seem to you to be reasonable and true, honor them; but if they seem nonsensical, despise them as nonsense, and do not decree death against those who have done no wrong, as you would against enemies" (68). Do not hesitate to act if convinced, but if not, refrain from persecution. Since God will hold us accountable for our behavior. Here Justin draws his extended apologetic to a pointed conclusion.

The Divine Mandates

His second apology is considerably more abbreviated. "Romans, the things which have recently happened in your city under Urbicus, and the things which are likewise being everywhere unreasonably done by the governors, have compelled me to frame this composition for your sakes."[5] "But that the cause of all that has taken place under Urbicus may become quite plain to you, I will relate what has been done."

"A certain woman lived with an intemperate husband; she herself, too, having formerly been intemperate. But when she came to the knowledge of the teachings of Christ she became sober-minded, and endeavored to persuade her husband likewise, citing the teaching of Christ" (2). "But he, continuing in the same excesses, alienated his wife from him by his actions."

"But she, considering it wicked to live any longer as a wife with a husband who sought in every way means of indulging in pleasure contrary to the law of nature, and in violation of what is right, wished to be divorced from him." But her friends advised her to continue with him, in hope that he might change. Instead, he left for Alexandria, and was reported to be conducting himself worse than ever. So that she divorced him.

Whereupon, he accused her of being a Christian. She, in turn, requested permission to arrange her affairs, and afterwards make her defense. Her petition was granted. Unable to prosecute, her former husband directed his assaults against the person who had been her teacher concerning the Christian faith. He persuaded a centurion to cast the man in prison, and to interrogate him on the sole issue of whether he was a Christian. And "being of a lover of truth, and not of a deceitful or false disposition, when he confessed himself to be a Christian, was bound by the centurion, and for a long time punished."

Then when brought before Urbicus, he was again interrogated concerning his Christian faith. "And when Urbicus ordered him to be led away to punishment, one Lucius, who was also himself a Christian, seeing the unreasonable judgment that had thus been given," astonishingly inquired: "Why have you punished this man, not as an adulterer, nor fornicator, nor murderer, nor thief, nor robber, nor convicted of any crime at all, but who has only confessed that his called by the name of Christian?"

While providing no defense for his misbehavior, Urbicus observed: "You also seem to me to be such an one."

"Most certainly I am," Lucius courageously replied. At which, he was also condemned to be punished. "And he professed his thanks, knowing

---

5. Martyr, *The Second Apology*, 1.

The Apologist

that he was delivered from such wicked rulers, and was going to the Father and King of the Heavens." Along with a third having come forward.

I, too, expect to be plotted against and fixed to the stake," Justin allows (3). Given the course of events, and threatening rhetoric. Since Christians were being made a scapegoat for all sorts of calamity.

Some will way, "Go then all of you and kill yourselves, and pass even now to God, and do not trouble us" (4). Why? "We have been taught that God did not make the world aimlessly, but for the sake of the human race; and we have before stated that He takes pleasure in those who imitate His properties." If, then, we kill ourselves, we are "in opposition to the will of God."

"But when we are examined, we make no denial, because we are not conscious of any evil, but count if impious not to speak the truth in all things, which also we know is pleasing to God, and because we are also now very desirous to deliver you from an unjust prejudice." Thus to preserve a pure conscience, as advocates of truth, which *is pleasing to God*, and out of a desire to curtail *unjust prejudice*. By way of setting a good precedent for others to emulate.

Consider how the angels transgressed, Although God "made the whole world, and subjected things earthly to men, the angels begat children who are those that are called demons; and besides, they afterwards subdued the human race in themselves" (5). In greater detail, "they sowed murders, wars, adulteries, intemperate deeds, and all wickedness." As further illustrated, they persecute the Christians.

Consider as well the names given to God and Christ. "But these words, Father, and God, and Creator, and Lord, and Master, are not names but appellations derived from His good deeds and function" (6). Hence, expressive of his character, and not to be treated lightly.

"Wherefore God delays causing the confusion and destruction of the whole world, by which the wicked angels and demons and men shall cease to exist, because of the seed of his Christians" (7). So that others are indebted to them for this reason. Likely giving rise to C. S. Lewis' observation that only God knows when more time will serve no legitimate purpose.

Consequently, we ought not to write off eternal punishment as a mere threat. Meant to dissuade persons from doing wrong, but lacking in substance. Again, as Lewis reasons, hell amounts to that which a compassionate deity provides for those who will accept nothing preferable.

Consider Christ as set over against Socrates. "For no one trusted in Socrates so as to die for this doctrine, but in Christ, who was partially known even by Socrates (for) He was and is the Word who is in every man, and who foretold that things that were to come to pass both through the prophets and in His own person" (10). Not "only philosophers and scholars believed, but also artisans and people entirely uneducated, despising both glory, and fear, and death; since He is a power of the ineffable Father, and not the mere instrument of human reason."

"For I myself, too, when I was delighting in the doctrines of Plato, and heard the Christians slandered, and saw them fearless of death, and of all other things which are countered fearful, perceived that it was impossible that they could be living in wickedness and pleasure" (12). "Be ashamed, be ashamed, you who charge the guiltless with those deeds which yourselves openly commit, and ascribe things which apply to yourselves and to your gods to those who have not even the slightest sympathy with them. Be converted; become wise."

"When I discovered the wicked disguise which the evil spirits had thrown around the divine doctrines of the Christians, I strive to be found a Christian; not because the teachings of Plato are different from those of Christ, but because they are not in all respects similar, as neither are those of the others, stoics, and points, and historians" (13). Thus not to overlook what persons hold in common, while maintaining the distinctive character of the Christian faith. Since error commonly consists of pairs of opposites. So that while we attempt to escape one fault, we fall prey to its alternative.

"And we therefore pray that you too publish this little book, appending what you think right, that our opinions may be known to others" (14). Since "by their condemning us, whom they do not understand, for an action which they say are wicked, they condemn themselves, so that there is no need of other judges." Bringing to mind Jesus' caution, "Do not judge, or you too will be judged. For in this same way you judge others, you will be judged, and with the measure you use, it will be measured to you" (Matt. 7:1–2).

In conclusion, Justin alludes again to Simon. Whose *wicked and deceitful doctrines* he despises. In hopes to set the record straight, and with the hope that he might be converted. "For this end alone did we compose this treatise. And our doctrines are not shameful, according to a sober judgment, but are indeed more lofty than all human philosophy" (15).

The Apologist

When Justin was subsequently brought before the magistrate, he refused to worship the gods. "Unless you obey, you shall be mercilessly punished," the magistrate threatened him.[6]

"Do what you will, for we are Christians, and do not sacrifice to idols," Justin resolutely replied. And so he and those with him were executed. Although his sage counsel lives on.

---

6. *The Martyrdom of the Holy Martyrs*, 4

Cost & Command

WHILE JUSTIN WAS AMONG the early Christian martyrs, Dietrich Bonhoeffer was one of the more recent victims. He was born in 1906 in Breslau, Germany but which now is in Poland. His father was a professor of psychiatry and an agnostic, as were his brothers. He decided early in his youth to engage in theological studies. When at fourteen years of age, his siblings insisted that "the church to which he proposed to devote himself was a poor, feeble, boring, petty bourgeois institution, he confidently replied: 'In that case I shall reform it!'"[1]

Having excelled in his studies, Bonhoeffer enthusiastically engaged in his pastoral duties. "But the rise of power of Adolf Hitler in 1933 disrupted his career. Two days after Hitler became Chancellor, Bonhoeffer opposed the Nazi *Fuhrerprinzip* (leadership principle) in a radio address—which was cut off before the end."[2]

Having a pacifistic inclination, he meant to explore this line of reasoning at greater length. Meanwhile, he took a stand with *Confessing Church*, by way of confirming the legitimacy of the church mandate. This eventually led him to observe that when you see a madman driving down the road, it is not enough to caution people to get out of the way, but you must attempt to stop him.

Whether he was actually involved in the attempt to take Hitler's life remains a mute point. He was certainly acquainted with some of those implicated, and in the waning days of World War II, executed. The attending physician appreciatively recalled, "In the almost fifty years that I worked

---

1. Bethge, *Dietrich Bonhoeffer*, 22.
2. Lane, *Exploring Christian Thought*, 206.

as a doctor, I have hardly ever seen a man die so entirely submissive to the will of God."[3]

Most memorable of his publications was *The Cost of Discipleship*. Qualifications aside, "Come to me, all you who are weary and burdened, and I will give you rest. Take my yoke upon you and learn from me, for I am gentle and humble in heart, and you will find rest for your souls. For my yoke is easy and my burden is light: (Matt. 11:28–30).

"The real trouble is that the pure Word of Jesus has been overlaid with so much human ballast—burdensome rules and regulations, false hopes and consolations—that it has become extremely difficult to make a genuine decision for Christ."[4] Consequently, it does not follow that all the criticism leveled against the church constitutes a rejection of Christ, as fostered by the spirit of the Antichrist.

"Cheap grace is the deadly enemy of our Church. We are fighting today for costly grace," Bonhoeffer adamantly asserts (p. 45). "Cheap grace means grace sold on the market like cheapjacks' wares. The sacraments, the forgiveness of sin, and the consolations of religion are thrown away at cut prices. Grace is represented as the Church's inexhaustible treasury. Grace without price; grace without cost!"

"Cheap grace is the preaching of forgiveness without requiring repentance, baptism without church discipline, Communion without confession, absolution without personal confession. Cheap grace is grace without discipleship, grace without the cross, grace without Jesus Christ, living and incarnate" (47).

"Costly grace is the treasure hidden in the field; for the sake of it a man will gladly go and sell all that he has. It is the pearl of great price to buy for which the merchant will sell all his goods. It is the call of Jesus Christ at which the disciple leaves his nets and follows him." Costly grace is thus expressed in graphic imagery.

"Such grace is *costly* because it calls us to follow, and it is *grace* because it calls us to follow *Jesus Christ*. It is costly because it costs a man his life, and it is grace because it gives a man the only true life. It is costly because it condemns sin, and grace because it justifies the sinner" (pp. 47–48). Above all, it is *costly* because it consisted in God giving his beloved Son. Hence, it cannot be cheap grace for those who embrace his gift.

---

3. Zimmerman and Smith (eds.), *I Knew Dietrich Bonhoeffer*, 232.
4. Bonhoeffer, *The Cost of Discipleship*, 38.

The Divine Mandates

"The call goes forth, and is at once followed by the response of obedience." Bonhoeffer observes. "The response of the disciples is an act of obedience, not a confession of faith in Jesus" (p. 61). Obedience to the one who calls, and for the purpose for which he is called.

"The first step places the disciple in the situation where faith is possible. If he refuses to follow and stays behind, he does not learn how to believe. He who is called must go out of his situation in which he cannot believe, into the situation in which first and foremost, faith is possible" (p. 67). Which recalls my own experience. When presented the gospel, there was much which I did not understand. But one thing impressed itself on me, the fact that Jesus said that he would not reject any who came to him. "If you can't trust Jesus," I mused to myself, "who can you trust?" And so I decided to follow him.

This is by way of affirming two propositions: "*only he who believes is obedient, and only he who is obedient believes*" (p. 69). So if one allows that he or she believes, we must urge this person to be obedient. Conversely, if expressing a willingness to obey, we must encourage the person to trust. If struggling in one regard or the other, then to focus on the alternative.

"When Christ calls a man, he bids him come and die. It may be a death like that of the first disciples who had to leave home and work to follow him, or it may be a death like Luther's, who had to leave the monastery and go out into the world" (p. 99). It may involve serving as a missionary in a foreign land, or raising a devout family. In any case, death to the former life, and life in Christ.

"Through the call of Christ men become individuals. Willy-nilly, they are compelled to decide, and that decision can only be made by themselves. It is no choice of their own that makes them individuals; it is Christ who makes them individuals by calling them" (p. 105). Accordingly, they become genuine originals, rather than duplicates of others.

Bonhoeffer next explores *The Sermon on the Mount*. "Let us picture the scene: Jesus on the mountain, the multitude, and the disciples. The people see Jesus with his disciples, who have gathered around him. Until quite recently these men had been completely identified with the multitude" (p. 117). Now they view one another across a divide, with mutual uncertainties.

Which again recalls my experience. Having returned from military duty, one of the young men with whom I matured inquired: "I hear that you got religion." I countered with the explanation that I had decided to follow Jesus. He seemed at a loss to grasp what was implicated.

"Jesus calls his disciples blessed in the hearing of the crowd, and the crowd is called upon as a startled witness. The disciples are called blessed because they have obeyed the call of Jesus, and the people as whole because they are heirs of the promise. But will they now claim their heritage by believing in Jesus Christ and his word?" (pp. 119–120). Or will they turn away?

For instance, "*Blessed are they that mourn, for they shall be comforted.* With each beatitude the gulf is widened between the disciples and the people. While the world keeps holiday they stand aside, and while the world sings, they mourn" (p. 121). Conversely, whereas the world languishes, *the community of strangers* is comforted by its association with the crucified and risen Christ.

"Up to now we must have the impression that the blessed ones were too good for this world, and only fit to live in heaven. But now Jesus calls them the salt of the earth—salt, the most indispensable necessity of life. The disciples, that is to say, are the highest good, the supreme value which the earth possesses" (p. 129). Reminiscent of Justin Martyr's commentary along this line.

Accordingly, "Flight into the invisible is a denial of the call. A community of Jesus which seeks to hide itself has ceased to follow him" (p. 132). So that the church mandate does not rule out social engagement, but requires it.

"There is no fulfilment of the law apart from communion with God, and no communion with God apart from fulfilment of the law. To forget the first condition was the mistake of the Jews, and to forget the second the temptation of the disciples" (p. 138). It is rather a *better righteousness* that hopefully distinguishes the disciple from those who opposed Jesus' teaching.

Bonhoeffer then touches on a number of related matters. For instance, "Anger is always an attack on the brother's life, for it refuses to let him live and aims at his destruction" (p. 143). For another, "No sacrifice is too great if it enables us to conquer a lust which cuts us off from Jesus" (p. 148). For still another, "Only those who follow Jesus and cleave to him are living in complete truthfulness" (p. 154). Finally, "The cross is the only power in the world which proves that suffering love can avenge and vanquish evil" (p. 161).

The Divine Mandates

"Love, in the sense of spontaneous, unreflective action, spells the death of the old man. For man recovers his true nature in the righteousness of Christ and in his fellow-man" (p. 178). In citing a quotation from the apostle Paul, "I live, yet no longer I, but Christ lives in me" (Gal. 2:20).

"Prayer is the supreme instance of the hidden character of the human life. It is the antithesis of self-display" (p. 161). A hiddenness that carries over into the devout
life as a whole. Resulting in a singular devotion, and a sense of freedom from worldly constraints. Thus doing away with anxiety.

"The path of discipleship is narrow, and it is fatally easy to miss one's way and stray from the path, even after years of discipleship" (p. 211). "There is no need to go about praying into the hearts of others. All we need do is to wait until the tree bears fruit, and we shall not have to wait long" (p/ 213). "If we follow Christ, cling to his word, and let everything else go, it will see us through the day of judgement. His word is his grace" (p. 217).

"Humanly speaking, we could understand and interpret the Sermon on the Mount in a thousand different ways. Jesus knows only one possibility: simple surrender and obedience, not interpreting and applying it, but doing and obeying it" (p. 219). This does not rule out reflecting on it and discussing it with others, but getting on with the course of discipleship.

The next segment of Bonhoeffer's text deals with those who would herald the gospel. Jesus "could not rest satisfied with the few who had heard his call and followed. He shrank from the idea of forming an exclusive little coterie with his disciples" (p. 223). Even though he was criticized for associating with *sinners*; that is, those who were religiously non-observant.

He summoned the Twelve to serve with him. While notably different, they alike responded to Jesus' call, which "transcended all their previous divisions, and established a new and steadfast fellowship in Jesus. Even Judas went forth to the Christ-work, and the fact that he did so will always be a dark riddle and an awful warning" (p. 227).

"The proclamation and activity of the messengers are identical with that of Christ himself. They were charged to proclaim the advent of the kingdom of heaven, and to confirm their message by performing signs. The message becomes an event, and the event confirms the message" (p. 230).

"Neither failure nor hostility can weaken the messenger's conviction that he had been sent by Jesus. It is, in the strict sense of the word, a *mission*. With this the Lord promises them his abiding presence, even when they find themselves as sheep among wolves, defenseless, powerless, sore pressed and beset with great danger" (pp. 236–237).

"The time is short. Eternity is long. It is the time of decision. If we have been true to Jesus in this life, he will be true to us in eternity" (p. 243). "He who offers a cup of cold water to the weakest and poorest who bears no honorable name has ministered to Christ himself, and Jesus Christ will be his reward" (p. 246).

The final segment focuses on the church in contest of discipleship, there is no other question—where today do we hear the call of Jesus to discipleship, there is no other answer than this: Hear the Word, receive the sacrament; in it hear him himself, and you will hear his call" (p. 253). By way of baptism, one "is wrested from the dominion of the world, and passes into the ownership of Christ. Christ invades the realm of Satan, lays hands on his own, and creates for himself his Church" (p. 256).

The Church constitutes one body. "Beyond the confines of the Church, there is only the old humanity with all its divisions" (p. 270). "To stay in the world with God means simply to live in the rough and tumble of the world and at the same time remain in the Body of Christ, the visible Church, to take part in its worship and to live the life of discipleship. In so doing we bear testimony to the defeat of this world" (p. 292)

"The source of both individual and corporate sanctification is the same, namely, fellowship and communion with Christ in the same body. Just as the separation of Church and world become visible only in their continuous conflict, so also does personal sanctification consist in the conflict of the Spirit against the flesh" (p. 321).

"Whom he foreknew, he also foreordained to be conformed to the image of His Son, that he might be the firstborn among many brethren" (Rom. 8:29). Bonhoeffer approvingly quotes. How is this to be achieved? "An image needs a living object and a copy can only be formed from a model God sends his Son—here lies the only remedy" (pp. 338–339).

"It is only because we are identified with him that we can become like him. Now at last deeds are performed and life is lived in single-minded discipleship. The follower of Jesus is the imitator of God" (p. 334). Recalling the injunction, Be therefore imitators of God, as beloved children" (Eph. 5:1). Thus concludes his engaging treatise on the cost of discipleship.

Shifting focus, "This book is not the Ethics which Dietrich Bonhoeffer intended to have published. It is a compilation of the sections which have been preserved, some of them complete and others not, some already

The Divine Mandates

partly rewritten and some which had been committed to writing only as preliminary studies for the work which was planned."[5] It was to have been his *magnum opus* (great work).

The edited text delves initially into the love of God, and the decay of the world. "The knowledge of good and evil seems to be the aim of all ethical reflection," Bonhoeffer reflects (p. 17). A quest that seems problematic from a Christian perspective, given the distinction created by man's degradation. Since "man's life is now disunion with God, with men, with things, and with himself: (p. 20).

Conversely, the New Testament approaches life not from "man's falling apart from God, from men, from things and from himself, but rather the rediscovered unity, reconciliation, is now the basis of the discussion and the point of decision of the specifically ethical experience. The life and activity of men is not at all problematic or tormented or dark; it is self-evident, joyful, sure and clear" (p. 26).

"The will of God is not a system of rules which is established from the outset; it is something new and different in each different situation in life, and for this reason a man must ever anew examine what the will of God may be. The heart, the understanding, observation and experience must all collaborate in this task" (p. 38). Recalling the admonition: "Do not conform any longer to the pattern of this world, but be transformed by the renewing of your mind. Then you will be able to test and approve what God's will is—the good, pleasing and perfect will" (Rom. 12:2).

Which invites an exploration of the church mandate. Bonhoeffer recalls a time when everything Christian was sorely oppressed. Subsequently, "Reason, culture, humanity, tolerance and self-determination, all these concepts which until very recently had served as battle slogans against the Church, against Christianity, against Jesus Christ Himself, had now, suddenly and surprisingly come very near indeed to the Christian standpoint" (p. 55).

Illustrating the unpredictable nature of culture from a Christian perspective. While affirming the distinctive character of the church, as a fellowship of the redeemed and in its role as a constructive social catalyst.

"Rarely perhaps has any generation shown so little interest as ours does in any kind of theoretical or systematic ethics," Bonhoeffer allows (p. 64). This "arises from the fact that our period, more than any earlier period in the history of the west, is oppressed by a superabounding reality of

---

5. Bonhoeffer, *Ethics*, 11.

concrete ethical problems." Such as gives rise to situation ethics, as a means of dealing with specific situations.

Om context, ""*Ecce Homo!*—Behold the man! In Him the world was reconciled with God. It is not by its overthrowing but by its reconciliation that the world is subdued. It is not by ideals and programs or by conscience, duty, responsibility and virtue that reality can be confronted and overcome, but simply and solely by the perfect love of God" (p. 70).

"Concrete judgements and decisions will have to be ventured here. Decision and action can here no longer be delegated to the personal conscience of the individual. Here there are concrete commandments and instructions for which obedience is demanded: (p. 88). Here then are divine mandates to be explored and implemented.

"The Church today is that community of men which is gripped by the power of the grace of Christ so that, recognizing as guilt towards Jesus Christ both its own personal sin and the apostasy of the western world from Jesus Christ, it confesses this guilt and accepts the burden of it, (p. 111). Being *gripped by grace*, the corporate fellowship embraces the cost of discipleship.

"Justification by grace and faith alone remains in every respect the final word and for this reason, when we speak of the things before the last, we must not speak of them as having any value of their own, but we must bring to light their relation to the ultimate" (p. 125). There is no ultimate without the penultimate, nor penultimate without the ultimate. In other words, "There is no Christianity in itself, for this would destroy the world; there is no man in himself, for he would exclude God" (p. 129).

This leads Bonhoeffer to reflect on the family mandate as well. In this regard, "Human marriage existed before the development of any of the other bonds of human society. Marriage was given already with the creation of the first man. Its right is founded in the beginnings of mankind" (p. 174).

"Marriages are not concluded either by the Church or by the state, and it is not solely from these institutions that they derive their title. The fact that a marriage is performed publically in the presence of the state and in the presence of the Church signifies no more than the civil and ecclesiastical public recognition of marriage and its inherent rights" (p. 175).

In addition, "Marriage involves acknowledgment of the right of life that is to come into being, a right which is not subject to the disposal of the married couple." Thus ruling out abortion in principle. As well as birth control as a consistent practice.

The Divine Mandates

It also precludes all that which shows disrespect for life. Such as in the instances of rape and torture. Likewise, with forced separation from one's family, or when deprived of some deserved honor. For in these ways the whole order of society is undermined.

"There are three fundamental attitudes which the life of the mind assumes with regard to reality: judgement, action and enjoyment (play and delight). In these attitudes man confronts in freedom the reality of which he himself forms a part, and he thereby shows that he is a man" (p. 186). These are to be cherished and preserved. Rather than compromised with the intent to achieving some social agenda. Recalling Bonhoeffer's own experience with the Third Reich.

Ethics revolves around the nature of reality. "For without God what meaning could there be in a goodness of man and a goodness of the world? But God as the ultimate reality is more than He who shows forth, manifests and reveals Himself, and from this it follows that the question of good can find its answer only in Christ" (p. 189). In this manner, to live in God's world—by means of his grace.

"In Christ we are offered the possibility of partaking in the reality of God and in the reality of this world, but not in the one without the other. The reality of God discloses itself only by setting me entirely in the reality of the world, and when I encounter the reality of the world it is always already, sustained, accepted and reconciled in the reality of God" (p/ 195). While drawing from the past and anticipating the future, this requires living in the present.

Bonhoeffer subsequently rejects the division of life into spheres, since there is a commonality in Christ. "The Scripture names four such mandates: labor, marriage, government and the Church. We speak of divine mandates because the word mandate refers more clearly to a divinely imposed task rather than to a determination of being (p 207). As a *task*, then to be undertaken as a creative exercise within the context of biblical instruction.

In greater detail, "It is God's will that there shall be labor, marriage, government and church in the world; and it is His will that all these, each in its own way, shall be through Christ, directed towards Christ, and in Christ. God has imposed all these mandates on all men. And it will not do to regard the first three mandates as 'secular,' in contradiction to the fourth."

If divorced from Christ, these mandates lose their divine character. "Labor 'in itself' is not divine, but labor for the sake of Jesus Christ, for the fulfillment of the divine task and purpose, is divine. The divine character of labor cannot be ascribed to its general usefulness or its intrinsic values, but only to its origin, its continuance and its goal in Jesus Christ" (p. 208). Conversely, while losing its impetus as a divine mandate, this does not negate its *general usefulness or its intrinsic values*.

The mandates of labor and family originate with Adam and Eve. "The divine mandate of government presuppose the divine mandate of labor and marriage. In the world which it rules, the governing authority finds already present the two mandates through which God the Creator exercises his creative power, and is therefore dependent on these" (p. 210). While it may legitimately supervise their activity, it must be with proper constraints.

"The divine mandate of the Church is different from these three. This mandate is the task of enabling the reality of Jesus Christ to become real in the preaching and organization of the Church and the Christian life" (p/ 111). Thus man "can gain access to this whole, without being town asunder by its manifold variety" (p. 213).

Ethics is manifest in the context of stewardship. Especially when one assumes responsibility for another. As with the parent for his or her offspring. Or the employer for those in his employment. In concrete situations and varying circumstances.

"From what has just been said it emerges that the structure of responsible action includes both readiness to accept guild and freedom" (p. 240). As for the former, embracing both commission and omission. As for the latter, "Responsibility and freedom are corresponding concepts. Factually, though not chronologically, responsibility presupposes freedom and freedom can consist only in responsibility" (p. 248). In other words, there can be no freedom *from* that does not embrace freedom *for*. Otherwise, it amounts to license.

"In the encounter with Jesus Christ man hears the call of God and in it the calling to live in the fellowship of Jesus Christ" (p. 254). This is expanded in terms of one's vocation. Recalling the pertinent injunction, "And whatever you do, whether in word or deed, do it all in the name of the Lord Jesus, giving thanks in God and Father through him" (Col. 3:17).

"The commandment of God is something different from what we have so far referred to as the ethical. It embraces the whole of life. It does not only forbid and command; it also permits. It does not only bind; it also sets free; and it does this by binding" (p. 277). Yet, it is ethical in a qualified sense. Since it results in commendable behavior.

No single instance of the divine mandates "can exclusively identify itself with the commandment of God. The supremacy of the commandment

The Divine Mandates

of God is shown precisely by the fact that it juxtaposes and coordinates these authorities in a relation of mutual opposition and complementarity" (p. 279). An *opposition* derived from their mutual exclusion, and a *complementarity* that repudiates competition.

"I honor my parents, I am faithful in marriage, I respect the lives and property of others, not because at the frontiers of my life there is a threatening 'thou shall not', but because I accept as holy institutions of God these realities" (pp. 280–281). When the divine mandates are incorporated into life and taken for granted. There being a pronounced sense of freedom, certainty, quietude, balance, and peace.

The term *mandate* is to be understood in a dual sense. First, the "conferment of divine authority on an earthly agent. The term 'mandate' must also be taken to imply the claiming, the seizure and the formation of a definite earthly domain by the divine commandment" (p. 287). Consequently, it pertains both to its divine provision and human utilization.

The second part of Bonhoeffer's reconstructed text is relatively brief. In this regard, he introduces the notion of *usefulness*, concerning its bearing on ethical discourse. Expressly concerning the promotion of the Decalogue, as a comprehensive guideline, and discussed at some length previously. Accordingly, the Church bears primary responsibility, along with the family and government. Moreover, it is coextensive with the proclamation of the gospel.

Moreover, the Church manifestly undertakes its task differently depending on its diverse circumstances. "The mission community, as a minority, will have to concentrate at first entirely on the preaching of Christ as a summons to the congregation, in order to open up a way for itself toward sharing in some kind of responsible work in the world" (p. 324). In more limited fashion, in anticipation of increasingly extensive labors.

"For the Church which is recognized by the state, and for the Christians who bear secular office and responsibility, the confession of Christ must include testimony to the commandment of God with regard to the state, economy, etc. But even the congregation in the catacombs will never be deprived of the universality of its task." Set forth as an eminent privilege, instead of a burdensome obligation.

In conclusion, "the right to speak always lies within the confines of the particular office which I discharge. If I overstep these limits my speech becomes importunate, presumptuous, and, whether it be blame or praise, offensive" (p. 371). Calling for persons to exercise discretion, so as to achieve a desired result.

Labor Mandate

LABOR IS THE FIRST of the mandates mentioned in Scripture. "The Lord God took the man and put him in the Garden of Eden to work it and take care of it" (Gen. 2:15). So things appear from the outset.

Several initial implications come to mind. First, this was God's intent from *the beginning*. Not an afterthought, of lesser consequence. Nor as a means for compensating for some earlier development.

Second, work per se is categorically approved. "It should be noted that even before the fall man was expected to work; paradise was not a life of leisured unemployment. Both *Enuma elish* and the Atrahasis epic also speak of man being created to work to relieve the gods. But the biblical narrative gives no hint that the creator is shuffling off his load onto man: work is intrinsic to human life."[1]

Third, that it should be at divine discretion. As with Adam, so with his posterity. If not in the *Garden of Eden*, then elsewhere. If not to tend the garden, then to be engaged in some other worthwhile activity. Meanwhile, inviting creative input.

Fourth, Adam was given permission to *eat from any tree in the garden*, except that pertaining to *the knowledge of good and evil*. Under penalty of death, accenting the seriousness of the offense. It was both an ample provision, and a gratuitous caution.

Finally, it was meant to solicit an appreciative response. For the opportunity of doing something of constructive nature. For the health necessary to carry out the related tasks. For the sense of accomplishment which

---

1. Wenham, *Genesis 1–15*, 67.

accompanies the enterprise. Ultimately for God's enablement and the delegation of responsibilities.

Now when Eve saw that the fruit of the tree was good, and also desirable for gaining wisdom, she ate of it and shared some with her husband. Consequently, God informed Adam: "Cursed is the ground because of you; through painful toil you will eat of it all the days of your life. It will produce thorns and thistles for you, and you will eat the plants of the field. By the sweat of your brow you will eat your food until you return to the ground, since from it you were taken, for dust you are and to dust you will return" (en. 3:17–19).

Circumstances would no longer cooperate with his endeavor. There would be adverse complications. Expectations might exceed accomplishments. Life's equation had been seriously compromised.

However, the labor mandate is not revoked. For better and for worse. Sometimes with a sense of fulfillment, but not uncommonly as a burdensome necessity. Recalling the sage observation, "There is a time for everything, and a season for every activity under heaven" (Eccles. 3:1). Hence, a time to labor and a time to rest from one's labors.

As noted earlier, Eve gave birth to two sons: Cain and Abel. "Now Abel kept flocks, and Cain worked the soil" (Gen 4:2). Both are depicted as legitimate responses to the labor mandate. Why? Since they constitute a proper division of labor. One that allows for a degree of specialization, which would otherwise be impossible.

An ideal which also implies cooperation between or among those implicated. Unlike the hostility that developed between the settled people and nomadic tribes. Leading to strained relationships, and outright conflict.

As previously considered, the Israelites were enslaved in Egypt. The "man-hours needed for the massive engineering and construction projects undertaken in the ancient world made the use of forced labor not infrequent. When the government projects proved too ambitious to staff with native people and prisoners of war, and too expensive to hire labor for, vulnerable groups of people would be targeted for forced labor."[2]

Qualifications aside, the Pentateuch resembles an emancipation proclamation. In the beginning, man was born free. With the exodus, the chosen people were delivered from bondage. Obedient to God, they were not to be subject to the disposition of others.

---

2. Walton and Matthews, *Genesis-Deuteronomy*, 85.

Labor Mandate

Slavery thus appears as a gross distortion of the work mandate. One that requires participation without fulfillment. As if the devil's alternative.

So it came to pass that the Israelites assembled at Sinai to covenant with the Almighty. "Six days you shall labor and do your work," they were informed, "but the seventh day is a Sabbath to the Lord your God: (Exod. 20:9–10). Two extremes are thus to be avoided. First, one must not allow labor to impose on the Sabbath observance. Otherwise, one loses a comprehensive perspective.

Accordingly, one cultivates life as a *sacred canopy*. As such, an occasion for persisting worship. With cognizance that we will assuredly be held accountable. Which eventuates in a life of welcomed service to others.

Less obvious, one should not refrain from labor. So it is that the rabbis reasoned that if one were not to work for six days, he or she could not properly observe the Sabbath. As a result, diligent labor is coupled with genuine devotion. Work and worship thus go hand in hand.

As would be expected, wisdom literature picked up on the labor mandate. "Go to the ant you sluggard; consider its ways and be wise" (Prov. 6:6). Although not aware of this exhortation as a child, I vividly recall observing the tireless activity of ants. Not only was I impressed by their industry, but their seeming ability to coordinate their activities.

Labor is perhaps best cast in specific instances. One of my mother's favorite sayings was "take a load when you go." While derived from carrying our dishes to the sink after eating, it came to apply to our otherwise sharing in the work that needed to be done.

My brother and I usually wiped dishes. Mother thought we performed this task better than our sisters, who seemed content with the impression. Mother, however, assigned them other duties.

Our obligations continued to expand as we matured. My brother and I soon assumed the major responsibility for our vegetable garden. This required planting, weeding, and carrying water from the river that flowed nearby. My brother was more conscientious, while I wanted to complete the task as soon as possible.

"I drew satisfaction from being able to make a contribution," I recalled earlier. "While modest in comparison to our parents' input, it served to share the work load. As a result, I was a better person than would otherwise have been the case."[3]

---

3. Inch, *Thumbs Up For the Family*, 100.

We were urged to choose our mentors carefully. On one occasion, mother became exasperated with my older sister. While singling out our maternal grandmother as a precedent for activity. Instead, my sibling opted for our paternal grandmother, who was considerably more laid-back. Which appealed to my sense of humor.

Raised in village culture, there was little anonymity. Accordingly, it was said that you did not have to signal a turn, since everyone knew where you were going. With few exceptions, our neighbors earned their livelihood through working in the woods, on a farm, or a combination of the two. The work hours were long and demanding.

My father inherited a general store. In the winter months, he would arise early to build a fire in our furnace. He then shifted his attention to the store, remaining there throughout the day, and well on into the night. On occasion he would refer to the store as his *jail*. Even so, he felt obligated to provide for the needs of his family, and seemingly derived pleasure from that realization.

Incidentally, he allowed the local pastor to purchase goods at cost. As his father had previously done. So while he did not attend church services, he was in some measure sensitive to the church mandate. Which implies obligations not only for those engaged in the fellowship, but others who cooperate in some manner.

Early memories aside, we pick up with Paul's pertinent correspondence. "We continually remember before our God and Father your work produced by faith, your labor prompted by love, and your endurance inspired by hope in our Lord Jesus Christ" (1 Thess. 1:3). *Produced by faith, prompted by love,* along with *endurance inspired by hope*—serving as a continuing reminder. Providing inspiration and an encouragement for intercessory prayer.

Love subsequently surges to the forefront. "As apostles of Christ we could have been a burden to you, but we were gentle among you, like a mother caring for her little children. Surely you remember, brothers, our toil and hardship; we worked night and day in order not to be a burden to anyone while we preached the gospel of God to you" (vv. 6, 9). Otherwise, they might have taken advantage of the generosity offered them.

As noted in an earlier context, love is expressed in the form of commitment. Rather than in a warm, fuzzy emotion. Or even in zeal, lacking righteous resolve.

Labor Mandate

"Make it your ambition to lead a quiet life, to mind your own business and to work with your hands, just as we told you, so that your daily life may win the respect of outsiders and so that you will not be dependent on anybody (1 Thess. 4:11–12). *A quiet life* implies tranquility, not inactivity. Such must be pursued relentlessly.

Mind your own business, and thus strive for excellence. Those who do so have little time to second guess what others do. As a result, they are not inclined to compound the problem.

The exhortation to work *with one's hands* is likely meant to repudiate the common practice of delegating responsibility to others, while enjoying a life of ease. Where one should, as in the case of the apostle, set a precedent for others to emulate. So much the more as one is given the opportunity afforded by favorable circumstances.

"If a man will not work, he shall not eat," subsequently concludes (2 Thess. 3:10). While Paul may have initiated the saying, "it was certainly he who made it part of the Christian view of labor. The concluding statement is not a statement of fact, 'he shall not,' but an imperative, 'let him not eat.' {Paul is giving the clearest expression to the thought that the Christian cannot be a drone. It is obligatory for him to be a worker."[4]

"We were not idle when we were with you, nor did we eat anyone's food without paying for it. On the contrary, we worked night and day, laboring and toiling so that we would not be a burden to any of you" (vv. 7–8). As the apostle observed earlier, by way of emphasis and encouragement.

Conversely, "We hear that some among you are idle. They are not busy; they are busybodies. Such people we command and urge in the Lord Jesus Christ to settle down and earn the bread they eat" (v. 11). He thus employs a play on words to contrast earnest labor with meddling in the affairs of others. If engaged in the former, then not likely to embrace the latter.

His *command* echoes the notion of labor as a mandate. Expressed in the context of his pastoral concern. For the benefit of all those implicated. Since what we do or fail to do impacts others.

Paul likewise calls attention to the relationship between slaves and masters, a situation more common today than most realize. Otherwise, it is similar in some respects to that between employers and employees. "Slaves, obey your earthly masters with respect and fear, and with sincerity of heart, just as you would obey Christ. Obey them not only to win their favor when

---

4. Morris, *The First and Second Epistles to the Thessalonians*, 88.

The Divine Mandates

their eye is on you, but like slaves of Christ, doing the will of God fro your heart" (Eph. 6:5–6).

Taking into consideration that voluntary slavery was widespread as a means of escaping abject poverty and starvation. Or when a person was not given the option. However, as previously noted, not as a preferable condition for labor.

Since many slaves embraced the Christian faith, it is not surprising that they were singled out for instruction. "For the majority of them, membership in the church may have been the only time and place they could experience equality and brotherhood. But belonging to Christ did not remove them from the world or lead to their emancipation."[5]

"And masters, treat your slaves in the same way," the apostle continues. "Do not threaten them, since you know that he who is both their Master and yours is in heaven, and there is no favoritism with him." Regardless of social status, God does not allow for favoritism. Therefore, all should be treated with respect and compassion.

Now this *labor of love* ideally eventuates in service. Although not out of necessity. For instance, the situation may not have been appraised correctly, leading to ill-conceived action. The recipient may also have misread the intent or failed to see its relevance.

"You know that the rulers of the Gentiles lord it over them, and their high officials exercise authority over them" Jesus allowed. "Not so with you. Instead, whoever wants to become great among you must be your servant—just as the Son of Man did not come to be served, but to serve and to give his life as a ransom for many" (Matt. 20:25–28).

Accordingly, Paul observed: "For I am the least of the apostles and do not even deserve to be called an apostle, because I persecuted the church of God. But by the grace of God I am what I am, and his grace to me was not without effect. No, I worked harder than all of them—not I, but the grace of God that was with me" (1 Cor. 15:9–10).

"Paul holds firmly to two things. One is the high dignity attaching to his position as an apostle (as can be seen) from several passages in his writings. The other is his profound sense of personal unworthiness."[6] Especially in light of his having relentlessly persecuted the Christian fellowship. Grace being the mediating factor.

---

5. Patzia, *Ephesians, Colossians, Philemon*, 91.
6. Morris, 1 *Corinthians*, 204.

Labor Mandate

Resulting in his toiling harder than the rest. Yet not to his credit, since it results from God's enablement. Without which, his labors would be useless. Such, however, was not the case.

As for select commentary, Francis de Sales allows: "Great works do not always lie in our way, but every moment we may do little ones excellently, that is, with great love." Dag Hammerskjold adds: "You have not done enough, you have never done enough so long as it is still possible that you have something of value to contribute." Hans Kung likewise observes: "Service of man does not replace service of God. But the service of God never excuses from the service of man; it is in service to man that service to God is proved."[7]

This calls for a reality check. "Torn out of a Christian context, the meaning of work has been distorted. Bereft of a vision of eternity and driven by an ever more acquisitive culture, many people have become obsessed with success in the here and now, resulting in a major shift in social priorities."[8] As cynically expressed by a friend, "The one with the most toys wins."

Conversely, Paul rebukes those "who think that godliness I s a means to financial gain" (1 Tim. 6:5). Such as were motivated by greed rather than *godliness*. While giving the appearance of pious devotion.

"But godliness with contentment is great gain," the apostle continues. "For we brought nothing into the world, and we can take nothing out of it. But if we have food and clothing, we will be content with that." Recalling the sage petition, "give me neither poverty nor riches, but give me only my daily bread. Otherwise, I may have too much and disown you and say, "Who is the Lord?" Or I may become poor and steal, and so dishonor the name of my God" (Prov. 30:8–9).

"For the love of money is a root of all kinds of evil" (v. 10). Resulting in theft, violation of the truth, hostile behavior, and the like. Thus driven by the wrong motivation to observe the labor mandate.

But to meet our own needs and that of others, in keeping with God's gracious purposes, and human need is exceedingly complex. Initially, there are those needs associated with survival. Such as involves food, clothing, and shelter. Bringing to mind the observation, "It is of no avail to preach to an empty stomach."

---

7. Sypes (ed.), *The Eternal Vision*, 401.
8. Colson and Pearcey, *How Shall I Live?*, 391.

Moreover, this recalls an occasion when I was talking with a social activist. "I have spent most of my life engaged on behalf of those who are said to be poverty stricken," he observed. "But I never realized the depth that poverty can take until visiting oversees." It was only then that he came to define poverty in terms of actual survival.

Then there are the needs associated with safety and security. Such as requires that we maintain a police force. In some instances, giving rise to a neighborhood watch association. Allowing persons to live without fear of having their homes invaded, and able to travel from one place to another without a pronounced risk.

This was a need addressed in traditional society by the extended family and clan. The stronger the tie, the more likely for success. A step removed from this social accommodation, one must devise alternative measure.

In addition to the need for security, one covets a sense of belonging and affection. Initially, my parents and sibling addressed this need. As did certain of my extended family. My grandparents in particular, since one set of grandparents lived across the road from us, and the other only a mile distant.

Later on in life, my wife and our children increasingly addressed this need. So I have graphically allowed that home is where Joan (my wife) resides. This allowed for our moving from time to time, whether in this country or abroad.

Friends also play an important role. Since most of my adult life has been spent in an academic setting, select students have contributed to our sense of belonging and affection. As have colleagues. Along with fellow church members.

There is also a need for self-respect and the respect of others. In this regard, "Speak up for those who cannot speak for themselves, for the rights of all who are destitute. Speak up and judge fairly; defend the rights of the poor and needy" (Prov. 31:8–9). Bearing in mind that the destitute are least likely to be accorded respect.

Self-respect is perhaps even more critical. Recalling that "God created man (generic) in his own image, in the image of God he created him, male and female he created them" (Gen. 1:27). As God's representatives on earth, humans are invested with authority to subdue the earth and reflect God's benevolent concern for it. If for no other reason, one should metaphorically speaking *stand tall*.

Labor Mandate

"A person's manner of interacting with other persons characterizes the way that one relates to God. Moreover, because God made humans in his image, God years to redeem those who have disobeyed him by providing the means for them to receive forgiveness and reconciliation."[9] Hence, human life involves a sacred investment.

Self-respect is enhanced when acknowledged by others. By polite discourse. While allowing for differences of opinion, and so on. As an apt guideline, "Do to others as you would have them do to you" (Luke 6:31).

There yet remains the need for self-actualization. Such as allows us to fulfill our potential. In a manner unique to each person. One with musical talent feels compelled to express his or her inclination. One with an urge to write characteristically hopes to have occasion to do so.

The emergence of these dispositions is usually associated with some prior satisfaction. For instance, if one has marked success in some endeavor. Or if commended by someone thought to be insightful. Suggesting the importance of assisting persons in experiencing gratification.

The notion of calling puts the quest for self-actualization firmly in the realm of the mandate. Accordingly, God is credited with both the provision and opportunity it affords. As if a gift waiting to be unwrapped.

All things considered, the Christian is called upon to provide a holistic ministry. One that speaks to the full range of human needs. As a means of implementing the labor mandate. Yet in cooperation with others.

Likewise, in the face of unrelenting obstacles. Even when plagued by apathy. No less than in the depths of despair. Recalling the familiar gospel refrain, "The God on the mountain is the God in the valley." Hence, ever faithful and sufficient to meet our needs.

Now leisure provides a welcomed counterpart to labor. According to conventional wisdom, "All work and no play make Jack a dull boy." *Jack*, whether by any other name. Lacking a time for disengagement and relaxation, we tend to become dispirited and depressed. Consequently, legitimate leisure is a good investment.

This is not, however, to approach leisure uncritically. There was no television to monopolize my time as a youth. Consequently, I became a bridge enthusiast early in life. It gave me pleasure to be able to compete with adults. I also enjoyed the conversation which resulted.

Our family frequently attended the movie theater. This was subject to mixed reviews. On the one hand, I especially enjoyed the cowboy films as

---

9. Hartley, *Genesis*, 48.

The Divine Mandates

an expression American mythology. The hero demonstrated his masculine qualities by his willingness to face danger. He would subsequently ride off into the sunset, so as to meet new challenges. The preacher characteristically play a supporting role, as well-meaning but rather inept.

On the other hand, there was much objectionable about this pastime. For instance, there was considerable violence. According to more recent studies, this results in two negative spinoffs. First, it encourages some highly impressionable individuals to engage in violent activity. Not most, but a few. Second, it creates a more general tolerance for violent activity.

Fast forward. Navigating the realm of academia is calculated to take a toll on an individual. Perhaps more for me than most, since I assumed the role of departmental chair for seventeen years, along with minimal instructional reduction. Then as vice-chair of the faculty at a critical period when anticipating an extended overseas assignment. Eventually in context of serving abroad, and adapting to unfamiliar cultures. While involved in extensive student counseling. Consequently, I attempted to link significant leisure time to family activities.

Left on my own, I managed team sports until my early thirties. I concentrated on tennis for the next three decades. Since then, I have been resigned to jogging three times a week. Team sports were especially challenging. They required discipline and cooperation. One had also to play by the rules. This venture appeared to be for the most part a constructive influence.

Tennis seemed especially appealing. Unlike team sports, it gave me an increased opportunity to develop my individual skills. I was seldom more content when engaged in this inviting activity. It also cultivated several meaningful relationships.

Jogging resulted from a process of elimination. It is convenient, and not unduly time consuming. Being highly predictable, it allows me to engage in prayer, and think my way through some perplexing issues. I also enjoy the experience of reflecting on our Father's world.

At this point, we invite the input of others. Tertullian was born around the year 160 at Carthage, into a pagan Roman family. He was educated in rhetoric and law. Sometime before the year 197, he became a Christian. For the remainder of his life he wrote expensively as an advocate for the Christian faith."[10]

---

10. Lane, *Exploring Christian Thought*, 17.

Labor Mandate

"The theater, gladiatorial combats, and contests between man and beasts were almost universal. Every city of consequence had prominent structures for them. Yet leading Christians without hesitation condemned the theater and the sports of the amphitheater."[11] Tertullian was manifestly no exception.

For instance, he protests: "who but God, the Maker of the world, put in its gold, brass, silver, ivory, wood, and all the other materials used in the manufacture of idols" Yet has He done this that men may set up a worship in opposition to Himself? One the contrary, idolatry in His eyes is the crowning sin."[12] This was by way of objecting to the idolatrous setting of the games.

He reasons that the Creator should be disassociated from the degenerate use to which creation is put. Idolatry is thus portrayed as a repudiation of God, along with an elevation of the baser instincts of humans. This gives rise to all sorts of evil enterprise. Leisure being no exception.

Having cited idolatry as a highly objectionable feature, "which alone ought to be reason enough for our giving up the shows. But we have spoken already of how it is with the places of exhibition, that they are not polluting in themselves, but owning to the things that are done in them from which they imbibe impurity, and then spirit it again on others."[13]

In particular, he faulted the incestuous character of the games. Then, in a more subtle fashion, the hypocrisy associated with the portrayals of love, wrath, fear, etc. His concerns were that others would emulate the behaviors they observed, and by implication, be condoned.

He also singled out brutality for reproach. "But if you argue that the racecourse is mentioned in Scripture, I grant it at once," he allows. "But you will not refuse to admit that the things which are done there are not for to look upon—the blows, and kicks, and cuffs, and all the recklessness of hand, and everything like that disfiguration of the human countenance, which is nothing less than the disfiguration of God's image."[14]

In greater detain, "Hippolytus declared that early Christian tradition did not countenance attending or taking part in chariot races. Augustine described and condemned the blood lust aroused by witnessing the gladiatorial combats. Under the influence of his new faith, the Emperor

---

11. Latourette, *A History of Christianity,* 244.
12. Tetullian, *De Spectaculis,* II.
13. Ibid., XIV.
14. Ibid., XVIII.

Constantine forbade gladiatorial shows and abolished the legal penalties which required criminals to become gladiators."[15]

With the waning of Christian influence in Western Civilization, neo-paganism has asserted itself. Allowing for all sorts of licentious behavior. While discrediting traditional values.

Creating in the process what may be graphically described as *cafeteria Christianity*. That is, such as are highly selective in their choice of Christian teaching. Opting instead to embrace cultural mores. The realm of leisure being no exception.

Which recalls a time when as a youth I witnessed a boxing exhibition. The two contestants were unevenly matched, and this became increasingly evident. At the sight of blood, the crowd was incited to cry out: "Kill him! Kill him!" The stronger of the two seemed willing to comply with their wishes. I was appalled, and later concluded that this was no place for a Christian to spend his or her leisure time.

Ideally, then, labor and leisure should not be competing entities. Since each fulfills a legitimate purpose. Providing they are in keeping with a high expectation of the divine mandates.

This brings to mind the apt benediction: "Now to him who is able to establish you by my gospel and the proclamation of Jesus Christ, according to the revelation of the mystery long ages past, but now revealed through the prophetic writings by the command of the eternal God, so that all nations might believe and obey—to the only wise God be glory forever through Jesus Christ!" (Rom. 16:25–27). So be it!

---

15. Latourette, *A History of Christianity*, 244–45.

Family Mandate

THE FAMILY MANDATE EMERGES shortly after its *labor* counterpart. No suitable *helper* was found among the animals Adam was called upon to name. So while he was sleeping, God removed substance from his side to create his female companion. She and she alone would serve in this capacity.

Accordingly, Adam observed: "This is now bone of my bone and flesh of my flesh; she shall be called 'woman,' for she was taken out of man: (Gen. 2:23). "The similarity in the sound of these two Hebrew words underscores that a man may find a true counterpart in a woman and vice versa. The close bond between them, enriched by their sexual differences, afforded them companionship and overcame loneliness. So together a couple finds fulfillment in life."[1]

"For this reason a man will leave his father and mother and be united to his wife, and they will become one flesh." This constitutes a major change in the social structure. One that allows the husband to take leave of his parents, and justifies his giving deference to his wife. Consequently, his parents are not permitted to invoke the commandment concerning honoring one's father and mother to prohibit this alteration.

Subsequently, "Adam lay with his wife Eve, and she became pregnant and gave birth to Cain. She said, 'With the help of the Lord I have brought forth a man.' Later she gave birth to his brother Abel: (Gen. 4:1–2). Sexual relations are thus allowed and encouraged within the bond of marriage. As are they otherwise prohibited.

Giving rise to the previously mentioned observation that there are three involved in giving birth to a child: God and its parents. All three are

---

1. Hartley, *Genesis*, 63.

The Divine Mandates

said to have invested interests, and legitimately so. This precludes taking the life of the offspring, or failing to instruct the child in the ways of the Lord.

Which recalls the observation, "Train a child in the way he should go, and when he is old he will not turn from it: (Prov. 22:6). Qualifications aside, early training will have lasting results. Exceptions do not prove to be the rule. But only if the parental training takes precedence over other influences.

"The family qualifies as the most venerable of our extensive social institutions. It also appears universal, allowing for modification to accommodate for exceptional circumstances. Moreover, it solicits a special affinity."[2] Giving rise to the notion that blood is thicker than water."

It also provides critical services for the perpetuation and enhancing of life. As noted previously, this speaks to a variety of needs. Encompassing physical, emotional, social, and spiritual features. While bonded together, each significant in its own right.

The family in traditional Middle Eastern society was patriarchal and extended. "It is usually headed by an elderly male, and its membership comprises all his sons with their wives and children, and the unmarried daughters and grand-daughters. The entire family resides together, in a cluster of neighboring tents in the nomadic camp, in a single house, or in several building clustered around a common courtyard in the villages and towns."[3]

Marriage within the extended family was preferred. Accordingly, Isaac admonished Jacob: "Take a wife for yourself from among the daughters of Laban, your mother's brother. May God Almighty bless you and made you fruitful and increase your numbers until you become a community of peoples" (Gen. 28:2–3)

Polygamy was customarily allowed, although practiced by only a small percentage of the populace (perhaps five to ten percent). Largely by the wealthy or when the first wife failed to give birth.

"In the nomadic tribe, its property is held in common; in the village, it owns jointly the land it cultivates; while in the towns if owns and manages jointly the enterprise from which its members make a living. Earnings are as a rule pooled, and expenses defrayed at the discretion of the patriarchal head."[4] Consequently, one's personal identity was forged in associa-

2. Inch, *Thumbs Up For the Family*, 1.
3. Patai, *Society, Culture and Change in the Middle East*, 21.
4. Inch, *Thumbs Up For the Family*, 3.

tion with others. Lacking such, gave rise in some instances to *non-persons*, thought to be something less than genuinely human.

Social conditioning was usually achieved informally, within the family circle. Children at an early age participated in the respective activities of their parents. When girls married, at or frequently before puberty, they were whisked away from their parental home. Their subsequent relationship with parents and siblings becoming remote, except in marriage between first cousins.

The nuclear family has largely come to replace the extended family in Western culture. It essentially consists of the parents and their children. It may accommodate other family members, if and when the need arises.

The mobile character of post-industrial society further reduces the importance of the extended family. Persons are more inclined to pursue individual vocations, which often require relocation. Thus even relations within the nuclear family structure become manifestly strained.

Parents often experience difficulty touching all bases, since they must take on responsibilities previously assumed by other resident family members. Accordingly the sense of family continuity suffers. Some enterprising person often assumes the role of a scribe to keep the family tradition alive.

"It would appear that the nuclear family now has a serious rival from, for the lack of a better designation, I will call *the anonymous family*. It is a make-shift operation, calculated to provide needed services—in lieu of some better defined alternative. The single parent home serves as a prime example."[5] Sometimes of necessity, but on other occasions derived from preference.

The single parent is not strictly speaking qualified to serve in the dual capacity of father and mother. A recent study identified four family structures: stable intact, conflict intact, single parent, and step-family. The single parent alternative scored lowest on the child well-being scale. The conflict intact and step-family scored higher. It came as no surprise that the stable intact scored highest. Recalling the sage counsel, "A word to the wise is sufficient."

The single parent structure can embrace two or more generations of unmarried or divorced persons. While these provide some of the advantages that accrue to the extended family, they do not as a rule result in the desirable male/female duality as role models for the children. This option is especially cultivated in a welfare society.

5. Ibid., 4.

In more subtle manner, urban street children may band together for mutual support. This can include living accommodation, shared income, and mutually agreed upon rules for behavior. If by any other name, this provides some of the services normally provided by the traditional family.

In still another instance, hospice care makes available services once attributed to the family. This may serve in conjunction with, or in place of, family resources. Each instance is in some way unique, and calling for creative input.

While current options might be explored further, these should suffice to illustrate the diversity now associated with family observance. As compounded still further in cross-cultural perspective. Which brings to mind the occasion when my father-in-law came to live with us. Friends were quick to commend my wife and me for what they perceived to be our selfless service.

However, my West African students appraised the situation very differently. "You are so fortunate," they assured us. They assumed that this would be a rewarding experience for us all. Conversely, they were critical of the practice of surrendering the aged to health care agencies. Insisting that such should continue to benefit from the loving concern of relatives.

From the perspective of a divine mandate, "Marriage is not, then, the effect of chance or the product of evolution of unconscious natural forces; it is the wise institution of the Creator to realize in mankind His design of love."[6] Hence, it is purposeful, not accidental. It is likewise a matter of considerable consequence.

Marriage was instituted as a means of procreation. Consequently, the birth of a child was considered a blessing from on high. So it was when Elizabeth gave birth, she appreciatively reflected: "The Lord has done this for me. In these days he has shown his favor and taken away my disgrace among the people" (Luke 1:25).

Current thinking has obscured this original focus, while fostering the goals of freedom and self-fulfillment. However, freedom implies obligation, and fulfillment should be understood in the context of God's gracious agenda for humanity. Otherwise, even the best of intentions amount to idolatry.

The family is also critical in the enculturation of the child. That is, to become familiar with and adapt to the prevailing social customs. Negatively

---

6. Pope Paul VI, "Human Vitae," 8.

considered, "In those days Israel had no king; everyone did as he saw fit" (Judges 17:6). Chaos resulted in inappropriate behavior.

Hebrew education was deliberately patterned after that attributed to God. Thus consisting of event plus interpretation. For instance, a place was made available at the Seder, soliciting the inquiry of the child. At which, the parent would associate it with Elijah, and was to prepare the way for the Messiah. Thus cultivating a lively curiosity, necessary the obtaining of wisdom.

Moreover, the parents were given to exhortation. In this regard, "Listen, my son, to your father's instruction and do not forsake your mother's teaching. They will be a garland to grace your head and a chain to adorn your neck." On the other hand, "My son, if sinners entice you, do not give in to them" (Prov. 1:8–10). Thus observe the divine mandate, and benefit accordingly.

Two related observations seem in order. First, "The more Christian the family becomes, the more human it becomes."[7] Life is enriched, rather than being inhibited. Not simply in select instances, but in a comprehensive manner.

Second, marriage can be summed up in two words: *love* and *life*. "*Love* not in some flimsy sentimental sense, but such as willingly sacrifices for another. *Life* not as a passing phenomenon, but as a meaningful investment in eternity. *Love* and *life* serve as two pillars on which to erect a solid foundation for the family."[8]

In still greater detail, J. Gordon Melton identifies fifteen recent developments that have conspired to significantly alter family life.[9] Such as should not be overlooked in a discussion of the family mandate. If for no other reason, as a reality check.

1. "The introduction of the highly reliable birth control pill made it possible for individuals to engage in sexual intercourse without the fear of pregnancy, thereby removing one of the major inhibitions of coitus outside marriage, and the same, within marriage." *Outside marriage* as a violation of the divine mandate. *Within marriage* not uncommonly as a means to circumvent an expressed purpose for which marriage exists. While not to the exclusion of other legitimate considerations.

---

7. World Synod of Bishops, "Message to Christian Families," IV, 12.
8. Inch, *Thumbs Up For the Family*, 7.
9. Melton, *The Churches Speak on Sex and Family Life*, xiii-xiv.

The Divine Mandates

When coupled with other artificial means of birth control, this has been acclaimed as *safe sex*. Which is obviously a misnomer, since sex can in any case result in pregnancy and sexually transmitted disease. Safe sex programs so-called show little statistical improvement, while driven by politically correct mythology. Although the effectiveness of abstinence programs continues to be debated, they assuredly do not indulge promiscuity.

2. "The rise of the feminist movement paved the way for new understandings of female and male roles which eschew the double standard previously practiced in sexual ethics and empowers women to make independent decisions about their social behavior." One that emphasizes the inherent equality between the sexes, rather than differentiated roles. As proposed confirmation, "So God created man in his own image, in the image of God he created him, male and female he created them: (Gen. 1:27).

In any case, the feminist movement plays to mixed reviews. On the one hand, it has addressed the inequities women have had to endure in traditional societies. On the other, it has failed to cope with some of the attending problems. Such as the much publicized home alone syndrome.

In this regard, the disparity of salaries between men and women is often employed as a means of agitating for better working opportunities. While there is merit to this observation, it characteristically overlooks the so-called *voluntary principle*. Especially as relates nurturing a family. Thus calculated to intensify the disparity, insofar as the wife is more often the caregiver.

3. Very "early adolescent dating without chaperonage, and exposure to explicit sexual scenes in television programs, movies, and advertizing have introduced young people to their sexuality much earlier than adolescents of previous time periods." In contrast to traditional societies, which as a rule retain supervision, and promote early marriage.

There was a time when sex was more of a private matter, discussed on select occasions. Now it is considered ad nauseam. In the process, it has become commonplace and trivialized.

Conversely, spiritual matters have increasingly been restricted from public discourse. Soliciting the observation of a political activist, "Children should not be told about God, since they are so impressionable." Worthy of note, she had no such misgivings about the discussion of sex in the grade schools.

4. "The delay of marriage for educational, economic, and personal reasons has provided opportunity and incentive to engage in sexual activity outside of marriage." A combination of factors being combined to violate

the family mandate. Lending not only *opportunity* but *incentive*. So that those less disposed are swept along by this adverse social trend.

In more graphic terms, this serves as the proverbial tip of the iceberg. Given the fact that contemporary society suffers from a lack of meaningful rights of passage. Lacking such, one is hard pressed to put life in perspective.

In contrast, traditional society greeted maturity with appropriate rituals. As was marriage. Precluding that which was thought inappropriate to the circumstances. Lending itself to stability and accountability.

5. "A new emphasis on the contributions that sexual intercourse can make to the establishment and nurture of fulfilling personal relationships has led many to argue against those who insist that coitus must be preserved for marriage and those who claim that the only purpose of sex and marriage is procreation." Whereas these considerations are not mutually exclusive.

This critique has erred in two additional ways. First, it has overlooked the accent on sexual attraction in traditional societies. For instance, the lover exclaims: "Oh how beautiful! Your eyes behind your veil are doves. Your hair is like a flock of goats descending from Mount Gilead" (Song of Songs 4:1).

Soliciting the response of the beloved, "Awake, north wind, and come, south wind! Blow on my garden, that its fragrance may spread abroad. Let my lover come into his garden and taste its choice fruit."

Second, it holds out too much for promiscuous sex. As such, it is inclined to reduce sexual activity to manipulation, void of a meaningful relationship. Thus focusing on the pleasure involved rather than intimacy with one's partner.

It appears that once wives began to enter the work force in sufficient numbers, their earnings might be projected in terms of a joint income. In exaggerated terms, the employer was able to get two for the price of one.

Moreover, expectations were inclined to rise with the increase of income. Things one thought to be an extravagance, now appeared to be a necessity. The materialistic case of society readily lent itself to this conclusion.

7. "A growing divorce rate has produced an increasing number of single parent families, usually with the mother as its head." Thus creating a need to manage felt needs outside the marriage framework.

This results in what has been graphically described as *serial polygamy*, the marrying of one spouse after another. Sometimes with less expectations. On other occasions, as a practical course of action. A trend that has carried over to a disturbing degree into the Christian fellowship.

The single parent must often choose between employment, to better the circumstances of his or her offspring, or giving them personal attention. This can be a very difficult decision, and subject to painful review. Although it sometimes leads to spiritual renewal.

\# 8. "The growing tendency for couples to live together without committing themselves to marriage has changed attitudes toward traditional values and sexual mores." Since persons are inclined to justify their behavior, while disparaging that which conflicts with it.

One can readily rationalize his or her behavior on the grounds of expediency. Whether in fact this is the case or not. Even when others seem to manage more successfully under similar conditions.

It is not that the traditional values have always achieved their purpose. Far from it! But they set a high standard. Then when persons fell short, they accomplished more than would otherwise have been the case.

\# 9. "Experiments in communal living in the 1960s and early 1970s encouraged alternative family arrangements." This appears to have been associated with the notion of *modernity*, in which it was thought that man had come of age, and was no longer held captive by uniformed ideology.

For instance, there was a time when I visited a newly formed commune. Those involved were highly optimistic concerning its outcome. The children of the respective families were housed according to age groups, and supervised by those selected for that purpose. The parents spent what was described as *quality time* with their offspring on the weekend. They were thereby able to escape the tedious demands of 24/7 on their time and energy.

In retrospect, most of these efforts seem to have been short lived. In a return to a more traditional family structure. And yet with a more lingering influence, in terms of priorities and means of achieving them. As with the substitution of public services to replace what had previously been in the realm of family.

\# 10. "A growing knowledge of family arrangements practiced throughout the world had forced people to recognize that the monogamous nuclear family is only one of many options available to human beings." More precisely, concerning the viability of alternative options.

Scripture, nonetheless, manifestly sets forth a monogamous ideal. As reflected in the policy statement, "that God intends marriage to be a monogamous, life-long, one flesh union of a woman and a man, who in response to God's call leave father and mother and cleave to one another."[10]

---

10. American Baptist Churches in the U.S.A. "Policy Statement on Family Life," 2.

While noting that "God gave them over to the sinful desires of their hearts to sexual impurity for the degrading of their bodies with one another" (Rom. 1:24). So that much of what we observe violates the righteous standards God imposes on sexual relationships. Along with adverse effects and lingering results.

11. "Historical-critical studies of the Bible have revealed that (it) sanctioned different forms of family life, thereby challenging the claim that God wills the monogamous nuclear family." As a theoretical reconstruction, at odds with traditional understanding.

The historical-critical methodology is itself highly suspect, reflecting a disestablishment agenda. It alleges to find diverse elements, said to be obscured by the narrator. Which appears highly presumptive, and calculated to be misleading.

It also plays off the alleged diversity found in Scripture against its unity. Opting for the former, it does not do justice to the latter. While allowing for the fact that one can err in the opposite direction. In this regard, it is also important to distinguish between what Scripture advocates and allows under certain circumstances. Divorce might be cited as a case in point.

12. "Historical-critical studies have also revealed that the Christian community, under the influence of Hellenistic categories, adopted a dualistic interpretation of human nature that puts an evil body against a good soul. Sexuality, being identified with the body in this tradition, was declared evil and to be avoided. The view contradicted the Hebrew roots of Christianity, which asserted that sexuality was good and to be available." With the implication that at least in incipient form this tension can be found in the New Testament scriptures.

This observation would be more appropriately applied to Gnosticism, which clearly departed from orthodox tradition. As for the former, it brought a dualistic mind set to its interpretation of the Christian faith, derived from its Hellenistic setting. Which incited a rigorous disclaimer by the early church fathers.

Qualifications aside, life is good from a Christian perspective. As such, it is meant to be appreciatively embraced. Providing, that is, that one lives according to divine instruction. Otherwise, it loses coherence.

13. The industrialization and urbanization of the world, accompanied by economic and geographic mobility for many individuals and families, has weakened traditional family and communal ties and the traditional

The Divine Mandates

authority exercised by these institutions over family matter and sexual morality." Creating discontinuity in search for meaningful continuity.

For better and for worse. For the better, because it provides opportunities previous generations could not have imagined. As with health services, access to information, and improved living conditions. As if the world were at our finger tips.

For the worse, since we are inclined to squander our natural resources. Thus impoverishing future generations. We also devise social contrasts that prove to be dehumanizing. Such as high-rise settlement projects that turn into urban jungles.

#14. "A growing emphasis upon individual freedom, especially in the personal realm, has challenged the authority of families, communities, and religious institutions have exercised in the area of sexual morality." While often imposing socially sanctioned (politically correct) ideals by way of public institutions and mass media.

Consequently, *individual freedom* appears as an allusive ideal. Since allowing for the input of *families, communities,* and *religious institutions* provide options that may otherwise be lacking. Along with the creative interplay of diverse influences.

"If you hold to my teaching, you are my disciples." Jesus declared. "Then you will know the truth, and the truth will set you free" (John 8:32). Otherwise, what passes for truth not only is lacking but distorted.

#15. "The publication of the Kinsey report, which revealed that many individuals did not adhere to the sexual mores of their primary institutions, led many to conclude that society needed a new sexual morality which reflected common practice." Thus assuming a pragmatic agenda, largely lacking moral considerations.

This represents only one of three evident general options. A second called for returning to the former ways. Not without merit, because it provides a means of drawing from accumulated wisdom. Recalling the observation, "Those who fail to learn from the past are destined to repeat its failures." Or benefit from its successes.

The third alternative requires an accommodation of former ways to new circumstances. Which seems more along the live of a covenant renewal, touched on earlier. In this instance, requiring greater creativity but with increased promise.

In conclusion, to live is to change. Such would seem inevitable. In contrast, legalism struggles to preserve the past. So as to maintain the privileges associated with the status quo, and provide security. But without marked success and with characteristically adverse results.

Change can be for the better for the worse, as Melton's observations confirm. So that we should not accept change uncritically. Especially when associated with so critical a consideration as the family mandate.

All of which recalls the marriage ceremony. The bride is commonly dressed in white, symbolic of chastity, and the groom in appropriate formal attire. The father waits to present his daughter on behalf of her mother and himself. The sanctuary accommodates family and friends.

"Dearly beloved," the cleric begins to read from the liturgy, "we are gathered together in the sight of God, and in the face of this company, to join this man and this woman in holy matrimony." *In the sight of God* serves as a solemn reminder of the mandate character of the ceremony. As such, it is in keeping with his gracious intent, and assured of his blessing.

Moreover, *in the face of this company* confirms the social character of the divine mandates. Consequently, the marriage contrast should be honored not only by the participants, but the community as well. Giving rise to its hearty approval and supportive efforts.

This man and this woman obviously envisages a monogamous heterosexual union. The cleric subsequently allows: "If any man can show just cause, why they may not lawfully be joined together, let him now speak or else hereafter forever hold his peace. In this regard, Clement of Alexander cautions: "But there is a time in which it is suitable, and a person for whim it is suitable, and an age up to which it is suitable."[11]

Prayer is an integral feature of the marriage ceremony. In abbreviated form, "send your blessing upon these your servants, this man and this woman whom we bless in your Name; that these persons may surely perform and keep the vow and covenant between them and may ever remain in perfect love and peace together, and live according to your laws, through Jesus Christ our Lord. Amen."

The participants are subsequently cautioned, "What God has joined together let no man put asunder." In Jewish tradition, it is said that when a man divorces his wife it is as if the very altar weeps. Now that the conditions have been met and properly affirmed, the marriage is then officially recognized. As an occasion for rejoicing and anticipated blessing, in keeping with the gracious purposes of the family mandate.

---

11. Clement of Alexandria, *The Stromata*, II, xxiii.

Government Mandate

IN BRIEF, GOVERNMENT INVOLVES the administration of public policy. As a divine mandate, it is validated in principle. Which obviously does not condone all that which is carried on by those in authority. Bringing to mind the sage caution, "Power breeds corruption, and absolute power corrupts thoroughly."

What might be described as *incipient government* dates from when humans began to proliferate. A more actualized government awaited the rise of regional authority structures. This was subsequently modified to allow for emerging empires embracing diverse people groups.

This transition brings to mind the patriarchs, and Abraham in particular. As touched upon in a previous context, God enjoined him: "Leave your country, your people and your father's household and go to the land I will show you" (Gen. 12:1). As one raised in a village culture, I can in some measure identify with him. I left familiar surroundings the day after my eighteenth birthday to serve in the military during World War II. I was only vaguely aware of what this would entail.

However, God assured the patriarch: "I will make you a great nation and I will bless you. I will make your name great, and you will be a blessing. I will bless those who bless you, and whoever curses you I will curse, and all people on earth will be blessed through you." Thus gratuitously fulfilling the government mandate.

A considerable number of people were implicated. "Now Lot, who was moving about with Abram, also had flocks and herds and tents. But the land could not support them while they stayed together. Quarreling arose between Abram's herdsmen and the herdsmen of Lot" (Gen. 13:5–7). A problem compounded by the fact that other people were living in the area.

So they took leave of one another. Lot opting for the Jordan plain, which had an abundance of water. While the patriarch was assured that his offspring would multiply like the dust of the earth. "Go, walk through the length and breadth of the land, for I am giving it to you."

God's covenant with Abraham remained in place with Isaac and then Jacob. So it was that the latter "lived in the land where his father had stayed" (Gen. 37:1) But when a famine arose in the land, the Israelites relocated in Egypt. Where they prospered for the time being. Then they were oppressed.

Here we encounter a more actualized form of government. "The necessity for control of the Nile was a factor in uniting Egypt and encouraging a tendency toward centralized authority. A strong government would sponsor a program of public construction to make the best use of the Nile"[1] So that government appears as a desirable means of accomplishing an expressed purpose.

The small states of ancient Egypt were united into two kingdoms: Lower Egypt and Upper Egypt. Even after having been combined under the rule of Pharaoh, the region was spoken of as *The Two Lands*, preserving something of their previous identity. "About 3000 B.C., when Egypt became a unified state, Upper Egypt emerged as the dominant power of the country and Horus became god of the combined empire of Upper and Lower Egypt. The Pharaoh was considered the incarnation and patron of Horus and was therefore considered a god in his own right."[2]

Consequently, the exodus appears as if a contest between Yahweh and the assembly of Egyptian deities. If not in specific instances, as plausibly argued, then in general. Thus demonstrating God's universal sovereignty, and the impotency of those who would challenge him.

Now the Mosaic Covenant is aptly described as *The Treaty of the Great King*. In which Yahweh sets forth the conditions under which the chosen people will enjoy his blessing. Or, conversely, solicit his disfavor.

Accordingly, when the covenant was renewed, Joshua admonished the Israelites: "Now fear the Lord and serve him with all faithfulness. But if serving the Lord seems undesirable to you, then choose for yourselves this day whom you will serve. But as for me and my household, we will serve the Lord" (Josh. 24:14–15). Reverence is thus joined with obedient service.

---

1. Pfeiffer, *Old Testament History*, 128.
2. Ibid., 133–34.

The Divine Mandates

Once settled in the promised land, there unfolded the turbulent times of the judges. "In those days Israel had no king; everyone did as he saw fit" (Judg. 17:6). Subsequently repeated by way of emphasis (cf. 18:1, 19:1, 21:25). "The Scribe thereby implies a lack of strong sustained moral and political leadership which would serve to bind the confederation of tribes together. Such leadership would make them strong enough to withstand the growing threat of the Philistines."[3]

With the arrival of the monarchy, greater stability proved to be no guarantee of righteous behavior. As touched on previously, the Northern Kingdom succumbed quickly to the influence of its pagan neighbors. While the Southern Kingdom struggled to maintain is covenant commitment, only to fall pry to the invading Babylonians. The previously privileged folk were carried away into captivity, leaving the remainder to struggle with chaotic conditions.

It came to pass that Nebuchadnezzar had a troublesome dream. "So the king summoned the magicians, enchanters, sorcerers and astrologers to tell him what he had dreamed" (Dan. 2:2). When they were unable to do so, he ordered that they be executed. When Daniel heard of this, he acknowledged: "No wise man, enchanter, magician or diviner can explain to the king the mystery he has asked about, but there is a God in heaven who reveals mysteries."

The dream consisted of a large awesome statue. "The God of heaven has given you dominion and power and might and glory. After you, another kingdom will rise, inferior to yours. Next, a third kingdom. Finally, there will be a fourth kingdom." Strong and yet brittle. "In the time of those kings, the God of heaven will set up a kingdom that will never be destroyed." When the government mandate has run its course, in compliance with God's gracious will.

Meanwhile, there came to pass the advent of Jesus as the Messiah. On one occasion, the Pharisees and Herodians set out to discredit him. As for the former, they reluctantly accepted Roman occupation, providing it allowed for their religious practices. As for the latter, they apparently were supportive of Herodian rule. In contrast to those who agitated against it.

"Teacher, we know that you are a man of integrity and that you teach the way of God in accordance with the truth. You aren't swayed by men, because you pay no attention to who they are," they consequently applauded him. "Tell us then, what is your opinion? Is it right to pay taxes to Caesar

---

3. Hamlin, *Judges*, 144.

or not?" (Matt. 22:15–17). They thus meant to put him on the horns of a dilemma. If he were to advocate the paying of taxes, he would lose support among the populace. If he were to protest the paying of taxes, he could be charged with rebellion.

Jesus was quite aware of their intent. "You hypocrites," he rebuked them, "why are you trying to trap me? Show me the coin used to paying the tax." When they brought him a denarius, he inquired: "Whose portrait is this? And whose inscription?"

When they acknowledged that it was *Caesar's* he enjoined them: "Give to Caesar what is Caesar's and to God what is God's." Leaving them to distinguish between the two. Having ailed in their attempt, they then withdrew.

It was obviously not Jesus' intent to allow for two separate spheres of authority. Instead, "Everyone must submit himself to the governing authorities, for there is no authority except that which God has established" (Rom. 13:1). A balance is called for, since "Paul makes clear that government is ordained by God—indeed, that every particular governmental authority is ordained by God—and that the Christian must recognize and respond to this fact with an attitude of 'submission.' But we should also refuse to give to government any absolute rights and should evaluate all its demands in the light of the gospel."[4]

The government mandate surfaces again in context of John's apocalyptic visions. For instance, a mighty voice exclaimed: "Fallen! Fallen is Babylon the Great! She has become a home for demons and a haunt for every evil spirit (Rev. 18:2). "Come out of her, my people, so that you will not share in her sins." Distance yourselves from its sinful practices.

"The merchants of the earth will weep and mourn over her because no one buys their cargoes any more." They will cry out, "In one hour such great wealth has been brought to ruin!" Conversely, "Rejoice over her, O heaven! Rejoice, saints and apostles and prophets! God has judged her for the way she treated you." Returning evil for good.

Then a heavenly chorus burst forth: "Hallelujah! For our Lord God Almighty reigns. Let us rejoice and be glad and give him glory!" For the good intent of the divine mandate eventuates in the consummation of his kingdom.

"All the above was obscure to me as a youngster. My first encounter with political activity revolved around the town meeting. It was a rather

---

4. Moo, *The Epistle to the Romans*, 809–10.

The Divine Mandates

raucous affair. There were efforts at humorous rejoinder. Tempers flared. The business was eventually expedited."[5] For better and worse, the results lingered.

My involvement in political life has been modest. On one occasion, I was urged by certain individuals belonging to the League of Women Voters to run for school board. It was then determined that they should not provide a public endorsement. So that without any significant visible support, I failed to win the election.

On another occasion, I enjoyed a cordial relationship with our state senator. Who encouraged me to express my views on pending pieces of legislation. But when I commented on two instances, he took issue on both. As a result, I was persuaded by his reasoning in one case but not the other.

Upon moving from New England to the Midwest, I was invited to attend a meeting of conservative political activists. But I was unprepared to their relatively extreme perspective, and was at a loss as how to respond. Incidentally, I have always considered myself as being somewhat right of center on the political spectrum. Consequently, in keeping with general orientation of the voting constituency.

In the course of my political journey, I came to what was at the time a novel idea as expressed by Reinhold Niebuhr. He reasoned that the adage *in and not of the world* could be applied in corporate terms. That is, while some Christians are legitimately engaged in church related vocations, others are meant to focus their efforts on social and political affairs. When coupled together, this suggests a strategic posturing. Moreover, it might suggest that churches should inform their youth not only of missionary opportunities but those pertaining to social engagement. By way of films, special speakers, assigned reading, and the like.

"Apart from vocation, all should take their role as citizens in a participatory democracy seriously. This includes being well informed, expressing one's views appropriately, and voting one's convictions. It no less invites prayer for those in positions of authority."[6] Information should include a familiarity with the critical issues, and the respective positions taken by candidates for public office. It also requires that one purge irrelevant considerations, often introduced by way of discrediting one opponent.

Not all ways of expressing one's views are deemed appropriate. For instance, shouting one's opposition while the speaker is attempting to set

---

5. Inch, *Thumbs Up For the Family*, 117.
6. Ibid., 118.

Government Mandate

forth his or her opinions or credentials. Such displays a manifest lack of civility.

Conversely, expressing a preference for a credible poll can make a contribution. Especially when taken in concert with others. Serving in some instances to offset the bias often encountered in the media, and persuading persons who are as yet undecided. Even when it is a minority view, which needs to be considered in a final determination.

Casting one's vote should also be encouraged. If for no other reason, to accept responsibility for what will transpire. As an inducement to be more responsible on a subsequent occasion. Which sometimes involves deciding between or among candidates who do not appeal to us. As the better of the available options. "I urge then, first of all, that requests, prayers, intercession and thanksgiving be made for everyone—for kings and all those in authority, that we may live peaceful and quiet lives in all godliness and holiness: (1 Tim. 2:1–2). For this is good and pleases God. *First of all* signifies a matter of prime importance. Without which our other efforts will prove largely ineffective. Reminding us of the critical need to incorporate God into life's equation.

It is not necessary to distinguish among the four types of prayer. Since the concern for others should be pervasive. Rather than confined to our own narrow interests, regardless of their legitimacy. While broad in scope, specific in application where this is feasible.

Examples of the universal scope of prayer are limited to prayer for those in governance, perhaps given the tendency for Christians to exclude them, "especially when rulers are openly hostile. Whether civil authorities are perverted or not they must be made the subjects for prayer, for Christian citizens may in this way influence the course of national affairs, a fact often forgotten except in times of special crisis."[7]

When Christians retreat from the political arena, they readily become an endangered specie. This was impressed on me in the wake of World War II, as explored earlier in the context of the writing of Dietrich Bonhoeffer. More expressly, with privileged information shared with me by Helmut Ziefle, who recalled his first-hand experiences as a youth in Nazi Germany. It was the intent of the authorities to reconstruct the Church along Aryan lines. Whereas the fall of the Third Reich cut short their political agenda.

The government mandate can be elaborated in various connections. For instance, Daniel Estes explores thee modes for assessing political

---

7. Guthrie, *The Pastoral Epistles*, 80.

leadership. First, he identifies *the political model*. In this instance, one focuses on the results that are anticipated. Qualifications aside, the end justifies the means.

The problems associated with this approach are legion. For instance, hindsight is as a rule preferable to foresight. Recalling the sage saying, "Act in haste, and regret in leisure."

Then, too, it is difficult to distinguish between what is simply expedient and a long-term solution. So that the preferable option may require a tentative resolution, with periodic review. In these and other regards, a person can be easily misled.

Second, he defers to *the integrity model*. This requires that one evaluate "the personal character of the political leader. If the leader has a commendable character, then he will be able to maintain a good role model for his constituents as he responds to the unpredictable challenges of office according to the patterns he has already established in life."[8]

While a viable consideration, it seems a part truth at best. For instance, a certain politician, whom I would prefer not to identify, was an exceedingly devout individual. However, he appeared quite naive, compounding the problems with which he had to deal. Most would seemingly agree that he should have taken a more realistic approach to issues.

Finally, Estes alludes to *the values model*. "It reasons that over time the public conduct of the leader will be marked by his personal character, which reflects his values. Therefore, the focus of evaluation is placed upon the principle criterion by which the leader sees the world, for this is the integrative center of his life."[9] Which recalls a time when I inquired of a Jesuit priest his appraisal of situation ethics, which focuses on the particular context. "It has value," he replied, "so long as one brings to the situation credible moral guidelines."

While an important feature in assessing leadership, there is no guarantee that the implications of one's world view will be aptly applied. Nor does it touch on the ability of an individual to take decisive action, nor maintain his resolve in the face of unrelenting opposition. So that, in conclusion, it would seem that one must make a decision based on complex criteria, and subject to reconsideration. Consequently, including other factors not cited above. Such as a pertinent expertise in the area of his administration.

---

8. Estes, "Psalm 101 and the Ethics of Political Leadership," 21.
9. Ibid., 21–22.

Government Mandate

D. Jeffrey Bingham explores the government mandate from the perspective of Irenaeus. From this perspective, "the State exists as God's creation for the purpose of ordering justice by penalizing injustice. Irenaeus also states that God has established these human rulers in a manner that fits those who at any given time are under their rule. There is diversity within the activities of the rules established by God."[10]

Justice is cultivated by penalizing injustice. "Do you want to be free from fear of the one in authority?" Paul rhetorically inquires. "Then do what is right and he will commend you. For his is God's servant to do you good. But if you do wrong, be afraid, for he does not bear the sword for nothing" (Rom. 13:3-4)

In addition, he applauds constructive diversity within God's benevolent design. Such as would take into consideration extenuating circumstances. Without preference for any. While employing all constructive means available.

In greater detail, Bingham introduces seven principles, derived from his reading of the insightful church fathers.[11] (1) Human government exists through the ordination of God. As such, it exists to serve his righteous purposes. And is not allowed to be usurped for personal gain.

(2) Christians are obligated to pay taxes to the government ordained by God. For credible purposes, and within reason. Otherwise, it amounts to corporate theft.

(3) Human government exists as a concession to humanity's refusal to fear God. As a means of compulsion, where persuasion fails. Then as a continuing reminder of human dereliction.

(4) Human government exists as a means to benefit humanity through the structuring of justice. Since what God ordains is for benevolent purposes. Thus calculated to assist humans in achieving their potential, while enjoying his blessing.

(5) The aims of human government to structure peace and justice are consistent with God's own benevolent, just nature and identity as Creator. In brief since God is good, he does good. Thus furthering *peace and justice* as a consequence.

(6) Human government conducts itself in diverse ways, both just and unjust. The diversity as such serves a legitimate purpose, but can be

---

10. Bingham, "Irenaeus and the Kingdoms of the World," 30, 32.
11. Ibid, 33; cf. Irenaeus, *Against Heresies*, V, 24, 1–3.

misappropriated for perverse purposes. So that those in authority must be held accountable.

(7) Although human government exists by God's design as a concession to human rejection of God, in order to beneficially structure justice, it does not supplant God's own sovereign dispensing of universal justice. Whether through the just conduct of the magistrates of God's condemnation of their injustice, he still dispenses just judgment to all. Consequently, justice will eventually prevail with or without the cooperation of the magistrates. As an encouragement to those disposed to further its pursuit, and a warning to those disinclined.

It can thus be seen that government serves a legitimate purpose. Even though it is often misappropriated. In any case, Christians are subject to a higher authority.

In more concrete terms, Jay Stack explores the role of voluntary service. "The Bible says that without vision the people perish, but I want to remind you that without people the vision will perish," he cautions. "In thinking about this conflict of vision, first of all, if we Christians are to make a difference in the arena of social issues, we must decide what issues we are going to emphasize."[12]

Without a vision the people perish. Recalling the observation that we are more drawn by the future than driven by the past. We draw from the past, anticipate the future, and act in the present.

Conversely without people the vision perishes. As when a cherished legacy is not passed on from one generation to the next. Or when persons fail to take into consideration the change in circumstances. Or in doing so they are reluctant to make necessary adjustments.

Persons must decide which issues take priority. Sometimes this decision is thrust upon one, so that it cannot be given proper consideration. Or given ample occasion, one may procrastinate. "As for man, his days are like grass," the sage observes, "he flourishes like a flower in the field; the wind blows over it and it is gone, and its place remembers it no more" (Psa. 103:15–16).

Some concerns are inherited. For instance, my paternal grandfather owned a store located near the Canadian border. This was at a time when there was extensive illegal liquor traffic. As an outspoken critic, he drew the ire of those involved. As a result, his store was torched. After which, he relocated.

---

12. Stack, "How Christians Can Have an Impact on Volunteers," 120.

His courage was recalled with appreciation within the family circle. As a precedent for others, whether in this connection or some other. As aptly stated, "One must have the courage of his or her convictions."

Some concerns arise from more immediate circumstances. "I am very, very grateful that my wife is very active in the crisis pregnancy center which our church sponsors," Stack subsequently allows. "I learned that it was one thing to preach against abortion, but it was another thing to be pro-life. I watched as we joined hands with some other denominations and came up with a home for unwed mothers—not just a crisis pregnancy center, but a home. We had several hundred people in our church volunteer to help in the home."[13]

Even one person can make a decided difference. If not at once, then with the passing of time. If not by him or herself, then in league with others. The persisting problem is that there are far too many watching from the stands, while too few are on the playing field.

"You want to know how Christian volunteers can change their society?" Stack anticipates the inquiry. "We can register folks to vote." He speaks from experience and leads by example.

"We can be politically active," he allows. "We ought to be; it is a sin not to be." In that *sin* is said to be any lack of conformity to the will of God. As touched on earlier, it can be a matter of commission or omission. The latter not uncommonly being the more subtle and grievous.

"We can give." Thereby coupling industry with generosity. The former providing the means, while the latter seizing the opportunity. In this regard, Jesus observed persons putting their offerings to the temple treasury. May affluent people made substantial contributions. "But a poor widow came and put in two very small copper coins, worth only a fraction of a penny" (Mark 12:42).

"I tell you the truth," Jesus solemnly declared, "this poor widow has put more into the treasury than all the others. They all gave out of their wealth; but she, out of her poverty, put in everything—all she had to live one." We thus are alerted that generosity is measured not by what one gives, but by what remains.

"We can hand out leaflets." It requires little ingenuity. A winsome smile is a welcomed asset. Cultivated in one context, it can carry over into another.

---

13. Ibid., 128–29.

"We can fight." As when arguing the merits of some course of action. Which recalls the sage observation, "All that is necessary for evil to triumph is for good people to do nothing."

"We can defend." Especially those who are more vulnerable. Sometimes as a result of a stereotype. Thus restoring dignity to the down-trodden. As a warning to those who take advantage of the misfortunes of others.

In conclusion, "To me a Christian volunteer is someone who knows, by the grace of God, that I'm going to cross the finish line. I just don't want to cross it by myself. I want to take someone with me." Thus giving the impression that voluntary activity is contagious, while in keeping with the government mandate.

This, once again, recalls my military experience. I enlisted rather than awaiting the draft. Along with others, as obligated citizens. Only later, when I had become a Christian, to wrestle the prospect of being involved in armed conflict. Then settling for something along the line of the just war theory.

It was some years later that I came across the journalist Tom Brokaw's allusion to *The Greatest Generation*. This came as a surprise that any knowledgeable person would have singled my associates and me for such distinction. It was not until I picked up on his rationale, that I could appreciate his perspective. In particular, he observed that this was a generation that accepted the task at hand, and saw it through.

What might be described as a realistic generation, lacking the idealism associated with those who served during World War I. Such as were unconvinced that this could serve as the war to end all wars. Consequently, a costly engagement with only limited results. But given the limitations, the courage to press ahead.

Granted that it involved danger, my service was not relatively threatening. But it was in this context that I witnessed violent death. I especially recall the wails of village women for the fallen. It seemed to express the depth of human agony.

I also remember standing by the flight line, watching the return of our planes following a bombing mission. Wondering if those who shared with me a weekly prayer and study meeting had survived. While concerned for others as well.

I likewise recall an enemy plane flying overhead, on what turned out to be for the purpose of reconnaissance. And wondering if this might be followed by combat aircraft. Should our pilots fail to intercept them.

Government Mandate

Many obviously failed to return from their deployment. My mother intuited that I would be among them, but did not share this until later. The grief of those they left behind also weighed heavily on me.

But it was not until some years later that I sensed how deeply I had been influenced. We were taking a group of students into the area where I had been deployed. Suddenly I began to have flashbacks, along with emotions long suppressed. Since there was no one who could identify with my feelings, I sat in silence.

My contribution to the war effort was meager. But I felt I had performed my duty, as associated with the government mandate. Not that I am inclined to armed conflict, but because it is sometimes thrust upon us. Or so it would seem.

Church Mandate

ANTECEDENTS FOR THE CHURCH *mandate* reach back to the dim dawn of human history and subsequently. "The first man was of the dust of the earth, the second man from heaven. And just as we have borne the likeness of the earthly man, so shall we bear the likeness of the man fro heaven" (1 Cor. 15:47, 49).

"The continuity existed because he who had been crucified was also seen, visibly and corporeally, after his resurrection; but his current heavenly existence also meant for Paul that there was obvious transformation. So with ourselves, he argues."[1] With implications for the corporate fellowship, since those who follow Christ are summoned into community.

We likewise encounter the provocative expression *our father Abraham* (cf. Luke 1f:73, John 8:53, Acts 7:2, etc). As that which "epitomizes the deep spiritual link every Christian has with the Jewish people. As we will point out, Christians are grafted by faith into Israel (Rom. 11:17–24), and through this faith commitment come to know Israel's father as their father also."[2] In this regard, "Understand, then, that those who believe are children of Abraham" (Gal. 3:7).

In greater detail, "By faith Abraham, when called to go to a place he would after receive as his inheritance, obeyed and went, even though he did not know where he was going. By faith he made his home in the promised land like a stranger in a foreign county" (Heb. 11:8–9). The patriarch, along with others, "were all commended for their faith, yet none of them received

---

1. Fee, *The First Epistle to the Corinthians*, 777.
2. Wilson, *Our Father Abraham*, xvi.

Church Mandate

what had been promised. God had planned something better for us so that only together with us would they be made perfect" (vv. 39-40).

Our attention is also drawn to Jesus' declaration, "This cup is the new covenant in my blood, do this, whenever you drink it, in remembrance of me" (1 Cor. 11:25). So while similar to the previous covenant, likewise distinctive.

Not only distinctive, but superior. "The law is only a shadow of the good things that are coming—not the realities themselves. For this reason it can never, by the same sacrifices repeated endlessly year after year, make perfect those who draw near to worship" (Heb. 10:1). In these and other ways, anticipating the church mandate.

"The Christian church was founded upon a story of people's experience with Jesus and a vision of God's reign in human history. Throughout the church's 'history' this story has formed and transformed, sustained and changed the community's faith and life."[3] *A story* concerning *peoples' experience with Jesus*. Such as when Jesus saw Levi sitting at the tax collector's booth. "Follow me," Jesus enjoined him, and he got up and followed him" (Mark 2:14).

Only two words, they speak volumes. As pertains to the cost of discipleship, the means of grace, and need for righteous resolve. Thus setting a priority with manifest promise. Coveted as such from one generation to the next.

This results in privileged corporate memory concerning salvation history. While those outside the fellowship characteristically retain a more limited recollection, not uncommonly distorted by alien influences. Although those with the fellowship are not altogether immune from such.

Along with *a vision of God's reign in human history*. "Is not life more important than food, and the body more important than clothes?" Jesus rhetorically inquired. "Look at the birds of the air, they do not sow or reap or store away in barns, and yet your heavenly Father feeds them" (Matt. 6:25-26). "But seek first his kingdom and his righteousness, and all these things will be given to you as well."

As a *vision*, in contrast to the current disparity. While experiencing an earnest of things to come. When the cosmic struggle will have ceased, and shalom is pervasive. Giving rise to eager expectation and ready service.

By which life is *formed and transformed*. Formed by way of Christian nurture, and transformed by the indwelling Spirit. "Therefore, it anyone is

---

3. Westerhoff III, *Living the Faith Community*, 27.

The Divine Mandates

in Christ, he is a new creation; the old has gone, the new has come. All this is from God, who reconciled us to himself through Christ and gave us the ministry of reconciliation" (2 Cor. 5:17–18).

Sustained and changed the community's faith and life. Sustained that which had been passed on to them, while applying it to changing circumstances. Both as pertains to their corporate convictions and consistent lifestyle. In a manner which is creative and compassionate.

Thus constituted, the church is meant to make the most of its opportunities. Which requires a continued vigilance. As to the needs to be addressed, and the means at hand. A certain congregation, set in place a procedure for ministering to the larger community. Individual members were encouraged to submit recommendations. These would be prayerfully reviewed, and select instances funded. As a rule for a limited time, until the ministry was self-sustaining.

For instance, one provided legal service. A critical need since the church was located in a high crime rate district. Youth in particular were often implicated. So that this became a welcomed means for Christian outreach.

Another instance concerned opening a Christian bookstore. Thus making available a range of Christian literature, and providing guidance in the selection of material. While alert to other needs that might surface.

A different congregation instituted a lay pastoral program. Those participating were initially given instruction, and subsequently supervised. Each was given a list of families whom they agreed to shepherd. They faithfully monitored church attendance as an indication of spiritual vitality, and were disposed to make telephone calls and home visitation in line with their ministry.

The efforts of a given congregation may be inhibited by public policy. In this regard, we attended a Romanian church a few years after the collapse of the Communist regime. On one occasion, we joined a group singing Christmas carols to some members of the congregation at their homes. When at one point they recalled a short time previously security had caused them to disband and flee down the adjoining streets.

On another occasion, because of increasing attendance, their sanctuary could no longer accommodate them. Were they to petition the authorities for a permit to build an addition, it would be refused. So under cover of darkness, vehicles would arrive to carry off excavated dirt from the area of the proposed church extension, and dispose it in the countryside.

Church Mandate

Eventually a foundation was laid, but the officials assumed that it was a playground.

Then, again under the cover of darkness, the frame of the extension was raised. Now alerted to the congregation's intent, the authorities took the senior pastor into custody. They refrained from executing him, since this might generate an uprising. Instead, they forced him to leave the country, with the threat that if he should return, they would do away with him.

As applied above, the church mandate involves both the invitation to *come*, and the exhortation to *go*. As for the former, "Come to me, all you who are weary and burdened, and I will give you rest" (Matt. 11:28). Given Jesus' disposition to comfort those afflicted. Rather than burden them with meticulous obligations.

As for the latter, go to herald the gospel. And to serve as the opportunity affords itself. Not reluctantly, but with hearty enthusiasm. While returning good for evil, and undaunted by opposition.

Without equivocation, the church is *apostolic*. In this regard, "They devoted themselves to the apostle's teaching and to the fellowship, of the breaking of bread and to prayer" (Acts 2:42). As for confirmation, "The community, the apostolic fellowship was constituted on the basis of the apostolic teaching. This teaching was authoritative because it was the teaching of the Lord communicated through the apostles in the power of the Spirit"[4]

Moreover, the New Testament was embraced as the repository of the apostolic teaching. Hence, it was authoritative in matters of faith and practice. Decidedly not one to the exclusion of the other. As such, it was vigorously defended by the early church fathers against heretical alternatives.

We are thus assured, "All Scripture is God-breathed and is useful for teaching, rebuking, correcting and training in righteousness, so that the man of God may be thoroughly equipped for every good work" (2 Tim. 3:16). *All Scripture* obviously allows for no exception. One is not free to be selective, resulting in what might be graphically described as a *cafeteria Christian*.

Recalling again Augustine's observation, "All truth is God's truth." So that Christians are encouraged to search for truth, while refining their understanding in the process. Then, by implication, what God says is in fact true. While what passes for truth in human circles is subject to error.

Consequently, Scripture serves a useful purpose. Initially, for the purpose of instruction. So that persons will be well informed, and not deficient

---

4. Bruce, *The Book of Acts*, 73.

in any regard. Then, by rebuking all that deviates from the truth. Assuredly for the purpose of cultivating righteous behavior. All things considered, so that *the man of God* will be equipped to perform the service of God.

If the church is genuinely apostolic, then also resulting in *unity*. Not uniformity but constructive diversity. In greater detail, "The body is a unit, though it is made up of many parts. So it is with Christ. For we were all baptized by one Spirit into one body—whether Jews or Greeks, slave or free—and we were all given the one Spirit to drink" (1 Cor. 12:12-13). So it was from the beginning.

So also it remains. "Now the body is not made p of one part but of many. If the foot should say, 'Because I am not a hand, I do not belong to the body,' it would not for that reason cease to be part of the body. But in fact God has arranged the parts in the body, every one of them just as he wanted them to be." So that each fulfills a necessary function, from which all benefit.

"If one part suffers, every part suffers with it; if one part is honored, every part rejoices with it." As when a person suffers an injury, which inhibits his or her activity. Conversely, when healed so that one can carry on his or her duties.

When taken together, the different parts constitute the body of Christ.. Hence, in Christ and in his service. Qualifications aside, as an extension of his own public ministry. With the prospect of accomplishing far more than we are able to do in a brief span of time, and without the assistance of others. Yet, as the result of his intercession and enablement.

"Are all apostles?" No. "Are all prophets?" No. "But eagerly share the greater gifts. Not those that solicit the acclaim of others, but such as provide a critical service.

"And now I show you the most excellent way." Here the apostle introduces the context in which the greater gifts are enhanced. "If I speak in the tongues of men and of angels, but have not love, I am only a resounding gong or a clanging symbol" (1 Cor. 13:1). Similarly with other gifts.

Love is patient, kind, does not envy, nor boast, or proud. It is not rude, self-seeking, easily angered, or keep a record of wrong doing. "Love does not delight in evil but rejoices with the truth. It always protects, always trusts, always hopes, always perseveres." It never fails.

"And now these three remain: faith, hope and love. But the greatest of these is love." "Even though love 'continues' in the present, along with its companions faith and hope, love is the greatest of these three because it 'continues' on into the final glory, which the other two by their very nature do not."[5]

If apostolic, the church is likewise *holy* (sanctified). Which is to say avoid the evils of this world, as a suitable means of achieving God's righteous purposes. As for the former, "Do not conform any longer to the pattern of this world, but be transformed by the renewing of your mind. Then you will be able to test and approve what God's will is—his good, pleasing and perfect will" (Rom 12:2). *Conformed* no *longer* to one's previous ways, but delivered from them.

Instead, *transformed by the renewing of your mind.* Given a new perspective on life. One embracing heightened opportunities and challenges. Along with the prospect of spiritual warfare.

Then, and only then, will one be able to accurately assess God's will. While cultivating a spiritual maturity. Accordingly, "When I was a child, I thought like a child, I reasoned like a child. When I became a man, I put childish ways behind me" (1 Cor. 13:11). Once dependent on others, now more capable of caring for oneself and being of help to one's associates.

"Husbands, love your wives," the apostle enjoins his readers, "just as Christ loved the church and gave himself up for her to make her holy, cleansing her by the washing with water through the word, and to present her to himself as a radiant church, without stain or wrinkle or any other blemish, but holy and blameless" (Eph. 5:25). Recalling C. S. Lewis' observation, "It is because God loves us that he seeks to make us lovable."

So it is that Christians individually and collectively should embrace holiness with divine intent. Not as an add-on, but as a consequence. With the anticipation of enjoying God's lavish blessing.

"Make every effort to live inn peace with all men and to be holy; without holiness no one will see the Lord" (Heb. 12:14). Of similar import, If it is possible, as far as it depends on you, live at peace with everyone. Do not take revenge, my friends, but leave room for God's wrath" (Rom 12:18–19). When couples together, strive insofar as *it is possible* to *live in peace with everyone.* Both friend and foe alike. Nor let the exception prove to be the rule.

Leave room for God's wrath, which implies that justice will be served. For only the Almighty knows when more time will serve no good purpose. "For the Lord is not slow in keeping his promise, as some understand slowness. He is patient with you, not wanting anyone to perish, but everyone to come to repentance" (2 Peter 3:9).

---

5. Fee, *The First Epistle to the Corinthians*, 161.

In this manner, cultivate holiness. By way of intention. By way of behavior. Thus both in thought and deed.

Finally, if apostolic, then *catholic* (universal). I have cited two illustrations on other occasions. "Once, kneeling in the prairie sand of South-West Africa, I celebrated the Lord's Supper with some Hereto tribesmen," Helmut Thielicke recalls. "Neither of us understood a single word of the other's language. But when I made the sign of the cross with my hand and pronounced the name 'Jesus' their dark faces lit up. We ate the same bread and drank from the same chalice, despite apartheid, and they couldn't do enough to show me their love."[6] They held out their children to him, and welcomed him into their modest huts.

"We had never seen each other before," Thielicke continues. We were separated by social, geographical, and cultural barriers. And yet we were enclosed by arms that were not of this world." As members of a universal church fellowship.

This, in turn, recalls a time when I was invited to participate in an ordination service in West Africa. At one point in the service, I along with other participants, enjoined to place our hands on the head of the kneeling candidate—for a dedicatory prayer. As I looked down, there were several black hands along with one larger white hand—my own. I was suddenly struck by the universality of the Christian fellowship.

It was not until some time later that I overheard the prominent evangelist Billy Graham, refer to *world Christians*. That is, those who are impressed by the universal character of the faith. So that it would appear that both he and I had become aware of its awesome character.

Balance is required in heralding the gospel in a cross-cultural setting. On the one hand, my culture is so pristine as to escape the critique of Scripture. While some are more amenable than others, all fall short. So that within the context of the universal church we can and should learn from one another.

Apart from the apostolic character of the church, the other characteristics are not genuinely within reach. There may be a unity of sorts, but not a unity in Christ. There may be a form of holiness, but not one enhanced by the Holy Spirit. There may be a syncretism without Catholicism. Only with the apostolic character of the church firmly in place does the body of Christ take shape.

---

6. Thielicke, *I Believe*, 131.

Church Mandate

There are predictable protagonists. Most obvious when an additional text is introduced, alleged to be divinely inspired. This characteristically takes precedent. While introducing novel interpretations of the apostolic documents.

In some instances a belated attempt is made to reconcile the conflicting texts. This is met with more or less success, depending on the willingness of the adherents to modify their claims. Such change as occurs is ordinarily represented as consistent with the previous posturing.

Whether generating a text or not, some claim prophetic prerogatives. This allows them to compromise Scripture in the process. Thus relegating the apostles to a secondary role concerning divine revelation.

For instance, some years ago a concerned co-ed mentioned that her pastor had informed the congregation that the biblical text was no longer necessary, since God had provided him as its mentor. In this capacity, he felt free to inform persons if they should marry or divorce. Even though he was reprimanded by his denomination, he retained the continued support of his flock. Which resulted in the fellowship being excommunicated.

Then the interpretive process may result in deviating from the apostolic tradition. Expressly when contemporary culture is given preference over biblical precedent. Not uncommonly in the context of situational ethics. Along with an emphasis on *relevancy*, which acts as a means for discounting textual considerations.

This has the effect of setting Christ over against culture. The former as represented by the apostolic consensus; the latter as differentiated in select cultures. The former cultivating constructive diversity, while the latter more given to diversity as such.

There is likewise the problematic role that tradition plays in apostolic continuity. If one thinks in terms of Scripture *and* tradition, it gives the impression that they are of similar, if not equal, consideration. Conversely, if Scripture *in* tradition—as expressed in Vatican II, then giving the impression that the former takes precedent.

Tradition as associated with the different denominations appears to be in decline. Whereas, it asserts itself more in terms of cultural preference. Not uncommonly encouraging a consumer mentality. Taking precedence over a service alternative.

Conversely, there have been concerted efforts to find common ground. For instance, the joint declaration concerning justification by Lutheran and Roman Catholic scholars. In this regard, "The Lutheran churches and the Roman Catholic Church have together listened to the good news proclaimed in Scripture. The common listening, together with the theological conversations of recent years, has led to a shared understanding of justification."[7]

One said to be consistent with the different emphases rigorously maintained in the past. Resulting in the Pope's approval, while allowing for the fact that some related matters were not considered. Thus paving the way for more amenable relations, and cooperative endeavors.

Which brings to mind the institutional structure of the church. "Throughout its history, from the very earliest years, Christianity has always had an institutional side. It has had recognized ministers, accepted confessional formulas, and prescribed forms of public worship. All this is fitting and proper."[8] It is also necessary and incumbent.

However, this can give rise to placing too much emphasis on institutional features—such as liturgy, at the expense of spiritual vitality. This results in what has graphically been described as *institutionalism*. Soliciting by way of protest: "From the point of view of this author, institutionalism is a deformation of the true nature of the church—a deformation that has unfortunately affected the Church at certain periods of its history, and one that remains in every age a real danger to the institutional Church."[9]

Consequently, the mandate might be said *to church*, since the community is obligated to construct and maintain a functional institutional structure. This may be represented as follows:

GOD
(who mandated the church)
FAITH COMMUNITY
(as recipient of the mandate)
INSTITUTION
(as the result)

In this case, the community is responsible to God for the state of the institutional church."[10]

Conversely, institutionalism alters the arrangement in the following manner:

7. *The Joint Declaration on the Doctrine of Justification*, 14.
8. Dulles, *Models of the Church*, 35.
9. Ibid.
10. Inch, *Why Take the Church Seriously?*, 108.

Church Mandate

GOD
(who is still as the course of authority)
INSTITUTION
(which now regulates communal life)
FAITH COMMUNITY
(now subservient)

In this instance, the institution usurps the role previously reserved for the faith community.

As a case in point, a certain young man was confused by what he read in Scripture. But when he turned to his pastor for clarification, the pastor enjoined him: "Don't worry about such things. Trust in the church, and it will see you through." Still troubled, he turned and sought help elsewhere.

As recognized at the outset, the institutional church consists of recognized ministers, accepted confessional formulas, and prescribed forms of worship. These invited our further attention.

Recognized ministers. With such in view, "Since an overseer is entrusted with God's work, he must be blameless—not overbearing, not quick-tempered, not given to drunkenness, not violent, not pursuing dishonest gain. Rather he must be hospitable, one who loves what is good, holy and disciplines" (Tits: 1:7–8)

"The term *blameless* serves as a comprehensive designation, which Paul proceeds to consider in various contexts. He also repeats the injunction by way of emphasis. The apostle is not thinking in perfectionistic terms. He had a realistic perception for what we noted in Jewish tradition as *the evil inclination*."[11]

Paul reasons that a person who cannot or will not manage his home well is an unlikely candidate for pastoral leadership. He perhaps looked on this as a training ground for more extended ministry. It would certainly seem to qualify.

Accepted confessional formulas. One may as readily err by a meaningless recitation of the creeds or a languishing lack of their use. If cognizant of one fault, we may retreat into the other. In any case, requiring that form not triumph over spirit.

"There is plenty of evidence in the New Testament to show that the faith was already beginning to harden into conventional summaries. Creeds

---

11. Ibid., 111.

The Divine Mandates

in the true meaning of the Word were yet to come, but the movement was under way."[12]

The golden age of the creeds is said to extend over the first five centuries. This included the Apostles, Nicene, and Chalcedonian Creeds. Their basic feature was to express the common experience of Christians. "Creedal activity continues at a diminished rate until the era of the confessions, about 1530 through 1700. The Augsburg Confession was issued in 1530, as was the first of the Helvetic Concessions; the Articles of the Church of England were agreed upon 1565, and subsequently revised in 1571; the last of the Helvetic Confessions dates to 1675."[13]

Eric Routley observes that confessions "differ from creeds chiefly in being characteristic of an age in which the unity of the visible church was precisely not the primary assumption. A confession becomes the manifest of a communion which wishes to make clear its difference fro another or from all others.[14]

Prescribed forms of worship. It seems initially that Christian worship conformed in large measure to that associated with the synagogue. This is not surprising, since Jesus frequented the synagogue—as did his early disciples. "The main scope of the Jewish synagogue was to have a place to unite the faithful for prayer and Bible reading. This purpose is also supposed by the Christian authors for their own synagogues."[15]

Prayer incorporated both praise and petition. Representative of the former, "Blessed are Thou, O Lord our King of the world, former of light and creator of darkness, author of peace, and creator of all things." As for the latter, any legitimate concern might be expressed—since God is interested and involved in all that pertains to life.

The Pentateuch was read on a regular basis, and excerpts from the Prophets and Writings on select occasions. However, reading from the Apostles soon came to dominate in Christian worship services. Along with observance of Communion. Associated early on with the *Lord's Day*, associated with Jesus' resurrection.

A homily might be included in the synagogue service, if it was thought that someone was suitable. Such as met the dual qualification of being well

---

12. Kelly, *Early Christian Creeds*, 13.
13. Inch, *Why Take the Church Seriously?*, 113.
14. Routley, *Creeds and Confessions*, 6.
15. Bagatti, *The Church of the Circumcision*, 113.

informed, and able to articulate effectively. The sermon became a dominant feature with the Reformation, with less stress on Communion.

Some traditions have sustained a more structured worship service, while others encourage spontaneous expression. Some churches have attempted to minister to a select group, although others provide increased variety. Mission churches characteristically carry over elements derived from their foreign mentors, coupled with cultural features from their own environ. All with the intention of responding to the church mandate: its Christ centered focus and constructive diversity.

Life

God endows humans with the means to observe his mandates. In this regard, the *Declaration of Independence* confidently affirms: "We hold these truths to be self-evident, that all men are created equal, that they are endowed by their creator with certain inalienable Rights, that among these are Life, Liberty, and the Pursuit of Happiness. *Life* is a prerequisite for the remaining endowments. Consequently, it should be zealously guarded and richly enhanced.

Since life is derived from God, it should be cherished—if for no other reason. Not put at unnecessary risk, nor neglected. With consideration of others, rather than squandered on self-indulgence.

While there were a great variety of creatures, only humans were created in God's image. "Ancient Near Eastern texts from Egypt and Mesopotamia use the phrase 'image of God' to mean an exalted position. Egyptian texts contain many references to the Pharaoh as the image of God. This title gave the ruler royal status and defined his role as the God's viceroy on earth."[1] In this regard, God instructed them, "Rule over the fish of the sea and the birds of the air and every living creature that moves on the ground" (Gen. 1:28).

Commensurate with his exalted position as viceroy, humans were endowed with such potential as is necessary to carry out their responsibilities. Recalling still again Mother Teresa's humorous observation, "I have no doubt but that God will supply whatever resources I need to accomplish what he has for me to do, but I wish that he were not so optimistic." Native intelligence readily comes to mind as a particular. As does creativity. Along

---

1. Hartley, *Genesis*, 53–54.

LIFE

with the ability to communicate with the Creator. In more subtle regards as well.

"From everyone who has been given much, much will be demanded, and from the one who has been entrusted with much, much more will be asked" (Luke 12:48). So that the welfare of humans and creation in its entirety is implicated. Coupled with human accountability.

Now in the middle of the garden was *the tree of life,* and *the tree of the knowledge of good and evil*—the latter having been considered in a previous context. "God generously granted man unlimited access to the fruit of all the trees, including the tree of life, which held the possibility of unending life for humans as long as they ate of its fruit. In the tree God provided the opportunity for patterns of obedience."[2]
Conversely, he cautioned that they not eat from its counterpart, lest they perish. Disobedience thus reaps a bitter harvest.

Explored in some detail earlier, Cain's murder of his sibling Abel, extended the life/death motif as a tragic consequence. When confronted with his disregard for life, Cain protested: "Am I my brother's keeper?" (Gen. 4:9). In brief and emphatically, yes!

Now it is Cain that worries lest someone retaliate, and take his life as well. But the Lord assured him that this would not be the case, and put a mark on him by way of protection. "It is astonishing that Yahweh did not sentence Cain, the first murderer, to death. Instead, seeing value in Cain's life, God graciously let him live. God does not give up quickly even on those who flagrantly violate another's life. God provides them continuing protection."[3]

Still, God does not ignore reality. As evidenced in the flood that engulfed the populace at the time of Noah. When human depravity made life virtually intolerable. But with the constructive intention of incorporating a decided change for the better. Out of a genuine respect for life, rather than that countenanced by an evil generation.

Fast forward. Jesus assured his disciples, "I have come that they may have life, and have it to the full" (John 10:10). Employing the imagery of *the good shepherd,* who "lays down his life for the sheep." Unlike the *hired hand*, who abandons the sheep when he sees a threatening wolf approaching. Since his concern is for recompense, instead of the welfare of the flock.

---

2. Ibid., 60.
3. Ibid., 84.

The Divine Mandates

Which would likely recall, "The Lord is my shepherd, I shall not want" (Psa. 23:1). In liturgical fashion: "He makes me to lie down in green pastures, he leads me beside quiet waters." *I shall not want.*

He guides me in paths of righteousness for his name's sake." *I shall not want.*

"Even though I walk through the valley of the shadow of death, I will fear no evil for you are with me, your rod and your staff, they comfort me." *I shall not want.*

"You prepare a table before me in the presence of my enemies. You anoint my head with oil, my cup overflows. Surely goodness and mercy will follow me all the days of my life, and I will dwell in the house of the Lord forever." Concerning time and eternity, *I shall not want.*

Fast forward again. "The most merciful thing a large family can do for one of its infant members is to kill it," advises a current advocate for population control"[4] With the intention of improving the *quality of life*, for some while at the expense of others.

Two analogies surface in this connection. Initially, in nineteenth-century England most villages were adjoined by a commons, land which could be used by the citizens of the community for grazing. "If the commons was used judiciously in a small village, individuals could gradually increase their wealth. But as the communities grew the temptation to over graze grew stronger."[5] Should one yield to the temptation others were inclined to follow.

Sooner than one would like to think the commons could no longer sustain its increased usage. Further use of the commons for grazing actually reduced productivity. If no preventative action was taken, the situation would continue to deteriorate.

The commons was meant to represent our environ. Accordingly, we have limited resources, and an ever-increasing population. The situation requires that we sharply curtail our population growth, given this line of reasoning.

So it is said that we must agree upon rules to keep our population in check. If this appears unlikely, the *elite* among us must take action. However this select group is constituted, while overriding the protests from the general populace. As illustrated in limiting the number of children that any given couple can birth.

4. Watkins, *The New Absolutes*, 81.
5. Pojman, *Life and Death*, 1.

The lifeboat analogy seems to be of more recent vintage, at least as associated with the Values Clarification Curriculum. In this instance, students are to imagine being in an overly crowded lifeboat—cast adrift in the open sea. There are scant reserves, compounding the dilemma.

It soon becomes evident that not all can survive. It remains to decide whose life shall be terminated. Since one candidate is elderly—having lived a full life, he seems a likely candidate. However, it turns out that he is a research scientist, who might make a discovery greatly benefitting society. So he is spared.

Cultural bias can be detected in the selection process. Clergy do not rate among the most highly valued, which suggests that their contribution is perceived as more marginal. Educators do better, perhaps in some measure due to their being involved in the exercise. Lawyers and salespersons do worse.

Meanwhile, the situation worsens. The craft is now taking in water. Some are incapacitated by trauma. Others feel compelled to throw off their natural constraints to preserve life, and deliberately cast those more vulnerable overboard.

Several observations seem in order. First, the situation is obviously contrived. Assume that we separate everyone into families of four. "We'll give each family a three bedroom house on a 50-foot lot, with a nice front yard and room for a garden in the back yard. How much land will we need? Well, the fact is that we could fit all in the state of Texas, with some space left over for the cowboys and oil wells."[6]

Granted, there are additional factors to take into consideration. Such as the means to provide food—apart from the family gardens, transportation, and the like. However, the situation is not nearly as desperate as the prophets of doom imagine. Especially if we were to take our environmental responsibilities more seriously.

Second, the persons implicated are anonymous. Which recalls the tragic case of Kitty Genovese. Persons were stunned at the time by her death at the hands of a stalker, while neighbors looked on from their bedroom windows for some thirty-five minutes while her assailant beat, stabbed, and left her for dead. Finally, a seventy year old woman belatedly called the police.

When asked why they did nothing, the observers' responses ranged from "I didn't know," and "I was tired," to "we were afraid." In addition,

---

6. Carr and Meyer, *Celebrate Life*, 11.

bringing to mind the clarification of a physician who employed prisoners for experimental purposes in Nazi Germany. "I felt no animosity," he confessed. "I simply did not think of them as anything other than guinea pigs."

Third, there is the temptation to *play God*. Accordingly, to usurp the divine prerogative to terminate life. As previously allowed, "The Lord gave and the Lord has taken away; may the name of the Lord be praised" (Job 1:21). Soliciting the approval of the chronicler, "In all this, Job did not sin by charging God with wrongdoing."

In a manner of speaking, human speculation replaces divine providence. After that, the law of diminishing returns characteristically sets in. As the sage observes, "When life is cheapened in some regard, it is cheapened in all."

Finally, there is the implication that those making the selection will be excluded from termination. If a class project, then the instructor and students. Which would seem to suggest, "Do to others what you would not have done to you." As such, the reverse of the Golden Rule.

Conversely, "Risks of life are often worth the goals of enhancing the quality of life for others. The martyr, the missionary to hostile territory, the settler, the witness of the truth all value something higher than their own life."[7] Not exclusively or primarily the quality of life for themselves.

All of which recalls a young couple, who were eagerly awaiting the birth of their first child. Much to their dismay, the child we severely handicapped, and would require continued assistance throughout life. The husband concluded that if there were a God, he would not have allowed this to happen. His wife struggled with the implications.

With the passing of time, a remarkable change took place. The husband reported that he had experienced love in a way he never thought possible. It was generated from their relationship with the child, and one another. Moreover, it seemed as if God were born again in his experience. His wife gratefully smiled her assent.

This should not come as a surprise. Since Jesus declared, "It is more blessed to give than to receive" (Acts 20:35). For in giving, we receive.

Advocates of population control generate a varied agenda, as the following will serve to illustrate:

---

7. Potman, *Life and Death*, 22.

Social Constraints

* Restructure family.

    a) Postpone or avoid marriage.

    b) Alter the image of ideal family size.

* Compulsory educations of children.
* Encourage increased homosexuality.
* Educate for family limitation.
* Fertility control agents in water supply.
* Encourage women to work.

Economic Deterrent/Incentives

* Substantial marriage tax.
* Child tax.
* Tax married more than single
* Remove parents' tax exception.
* Additional taxes on parents with more than 1 or 2 children in school.

Social Controls

*Compulsory abortion of out-of-wedlock pregnancies.

* Compulsory sterilization of all who have two children except for a few who would be allowed three.

*Confine childbearing to only a limited number of adults.[8]

In less detail, Planned Parenthood of America concludes that universal reproductive freedom is perhaps the most critical step in solving the problem of hunger, deprivation and hopelessness associated with poverty, and the depletion of our natural resources. *Universal reproductive freedom* embraces making contraception, abortion, and sterilization readily available to all. While anticipating that those failing to comply may have to be

---

8. Carr and Meyer, *Celebrate Life*, 14–15.

coerced, with a calculated disregard with the sanctity of life as an overriding consideration.

We are thus encouraged to explore the issue of abortion in greater detail. Abortion, although widely practiced, was considered immoral and illegal in most modern western societies until recently. "The 1960s brought increasing activism in favor of legalizing abortion. Initially, the motives were to help women who were victims of rape or incest, and those who carried deformed babies, as well as to eliminate the dangers of illegal abortion. Later, the goal of the advocates became abortion-on-demand for any reason at all."[9]

The Supreme Court's *Roe v. Wade* decision ruled that the states could not forbid abortions in the first trimester of pregnancy, but are allowed to regulate the procedure. In the final trimester, the states were permitted to prohibit abortion—except when the life or health of the woman was at stake. *Health* came to be understood as synonymous with the person's well-being. Since an unwanted pregnancy would increase stress, abortion on demand resulted. Overlooked in this regard was the emotional fallout that not uncommonly lingered from the guilt feelings associated with abortion of the fetus.

It is said that more than twenty million abortions have been performed since the 1973 decision. This runs counter not only to those within the Judeo-Christian tradition, but the general public. Accordingly, former President Clinton observed that most Americans want abortion to be safe, legal, and seldom. The current practice, while attempting to guarantee the first two of these goals, makes a mockery of the third.

Several positions emerge in context of the abortion debate. Some Christian denominations oppose artificial means for birth control. Qualifications aside, allowing for natural means—such as abstaining from intercourse. Others advocate discretion in the use of means. Taking into consideration God's injunction that humans should proliferate (cf. Gen. 1:28).

Once life is conceived, some insist that it is sacred from that juncture. Thus ruling out abortion or allowing it only in extreme instances. Such as when the woman's life is seriously at risk, in instances of rape, or when the fetus is deformed in some manner.

While others draw a distinction between biological life and when the fetus can be considered a *person*. Since this distinction appears more or

---

9. Orr et al., *Life and Death Decisions*, 48–49.

LIFE

less arbitrary, it allows for considerable room for application. While being subject to concerned criticism.

It also encourages the use of *quickening* as a criterion. That is, when the mother first feels the fetus move. However, the appeal of this alternative has diminished, so that it remains a live option for only a few.

Viability has been a more resilient benchmark. As relates too the ability of the fetus to fend for itself. If given the opportunity. Which seems more in keeping with the original intent of the Supreme Court ruling. Although the Court has been reluctant to spell out what this implies. Short of more definitive guidelines, the carnage continues undaunted.

Experience provides yet another alternative. In this regard, it is said that the right to life must embrace the ability to perceive, suffer, and remember. It is further alleged that the fetus is unable to do any of these, and so need not be guaranteed life.

This view is subject to two primary objections. First, if strictly interpreted, it might include infants as well. Since their perception is limited, and their memory immature. Second, there is ample evidence that the fetus experiences both pleasure and pain.

Birth is a more plausible criterion. Since it is at this point that the offspring takes on a separate existence. However, there does not seem to be any change in its actual composition.

Partial-birth abortion highlights the issue. In this instance, the delivery is inhibited so that the abortion can be performed. This appears to be the most objectionable instance of abortion, since it is so closely associated with infanticide.

By way of summary, the pro-choice advocates submit four arguments to validate their position. Initially, there is *relativism*. It is alleged that abortion is strictly an individual matter. No one should be coerced into having unwanted children. Morality, from this perspective, is a private concern.

If, however, we were consistent, this would rule out the protection guaranteed to others. Unless, of course, there is some compelling reason for excluding the fetus from consideration. If this is not the case, and the burden of proof lies with the pro-choice advocates, because the wanton taking of life amounts to mass extermination.

The right to privacy is likewise set forth as a rationale. Accordingly, The National Organization of Women insists that a woman has an absolute right to her own body. Since the fetus is dependent, she can dispose of it if she wishes to do so. If this involves abortion, it is within her prerogative.

The Divine Mandates

Thus recalling that crisis pregnancy centers report that persons using their services characteristically allow that they lack the information necessary for making an intelligent decision. As if to suggest that society conspires to advocate abortion.

Conversely, we do not have absolute rights, in the sense that it precludes the consideration of others. As popularly expressed, "Your freedom stops where my nose begins." In addition, one's behavior is considered a matter of public concern, in that it impacts society—whether for better or worse.

As touched on earlier, *the quality of life* emerges as a consideration. Such as given the prospect of a deformed or retarded child, when unable to provide for the needs of the offspring, in the case of teenage pregnancy, and the like. As explored previously, the specter of over-population provides an added consideration.

In brief, while the quality of life is a legitimate concern, it ought not to be used as an excuse to sanction irresponsible and immoral behavior. In this regard, the lesser good should not excuse neglect of the greater good.

Finally, as to what constitutes a *person*. In particular, the mother is given a status that not only exceeds that of the fetus, but strips it of any inherent rights. Only a fine line distinguishes it from infanticide.

The burden of proof seems repeatedly to lie with the pro-choice advocates. Lacking a more compelling rationale, their claim seems unconvincing. While legitimate concerns can be addressed in various ways.

All the above recalls a provocative story concerning the famed violinist Yitzak Perlman. As a child, he was stricken with polio, leaving him severely incapacitated. He wore braces on both legs, and could walk only with the assistance of crutches.

One evening, he was to give a concert. As soon as he appeared on stage, the audience enthusiastically applauded him, and waited expectantly for his performance. No sooner had he begun to play than one of his violin strings snapped with a sound resembling a gunshot. He could have halted the performance, and replaced the string. Instead, he hesitated and then signaled the conductor to continue. He proceeded to improvise with the remaining strings on his instrument.

When he had finished, the audience sat for a moment in stunned silence. Then they rose to their feet, and cheered wildly. They realized that they had witnessed an extraordinary display of skill and ingenuity.

Life

Perlman raised his bow to signal for silence. "Sometimes it is the artist's task to find out how much beautiful music you can still make with what you have left," he observed. While making reference to his impaired instrument, it was not less applicable to his crippled body. The world is a better place for such courage, fortitude, and artistry.

How tragic to realize that many gifted persons, let alone those less so, who were never allowed to achieve their potential. Perhaps because of some deficiency diagnosed in the fetus. Otherwise, because of economic considerations. Worse yet, simply because giving birth would create some inconvenience.

We now consider the sanctity of life in a much different setting, with the prevalent and threatening practice of terrorism. It consists of violence meant to promote social and political change. It has come to especially apply to purposely inflict civilian casualties. As an example, the detonation of a bomb in a crowded restaurant or shopping district. Sometimes identified as *soft targets,* as set over against military or otherwise secure installations.

Terrorism is not a new phenomenon. For instance, the Jewish Sicari sought to intimidate those compromising with Roman occupation. Their favorite weapon was the *sica,* a short dagger, which they used to execute those deemed apostate. Then, too, to caution others not to yield to the temptation. Such killings usually occurred during daylight and in public for maximum effectiveness.

Terrorism now influences events on the international state to a degree in excess of previous times. As highlighted by the attack on the New York Trade Towers, recalled by the idiomatic reference to 9/11. "Since then, in the United States at least, terrorism has largely been equated to the threat posed by al Queda—a threat inflamed not only by the spectacular and deadly nature of the Sept. 11 attacks themselves, but by the fear that future strikes might be even more deadly and employ weapons of mass destruction"[10]

Two planes loaded with passengers collided with the twin trade towers, causing their destruction. A third crashed into the Pentagon, and a fourth in an open field in rural Pennsylvania. Its target may have been the Capital or White House. Todd Beamer was one of the passengers who perished in its futile effort. A graduate of Wheaton College, Wheaton, Illinois, where I taught for twenty-four years, so as to more readily identify with him.

---

10. Center for Defense Information, *A Brief History of Terrorism,* 7.

The Divine Mandates

Beamer, age 32, was an Oracle Inc. executive at the time. Lesa Jefferson a GET supervisor, talked with him for about thirteen minutes before the plane went down. He informed her that he and his companions were going to attempt to thwart the efforts of the hijackers. He had her promise to pass on the information to his wife and children.

Jefferson could hear shouts and commotion. After which, Beamer asked her to have prayer with him. They recited the Twenty-Third Psalm together, concerning the Lord being their shepherd. Thus celebrating life in context of tragic events unfolding. He then dropped the phone, leaving the line open. The last thing Jefferson heard was his characteristic expression, "Let's role."

"Just knowing that when the crisis came up he maintained the same character we all knew; it's a testament to what real faith means," his wife concluded. Yes, indeed!

Surveying the context the National Guard had prior to 9/11, it began the process of restructuring its units to play a more active role in homeland security. In light of 9/11, the process took on greater urgency. Under the revised plan, a number of heavily armored and mechanized brigades would be converted to motorized infantry. In military jargon, they would thus be classified as *Mobile Light Brigades*. These would be focused on the low end of the combat spectrum, ranging from homeland security to higher intensity conflict.

The second initiative consisted of expanding engineer, chemical, and military police forces. It was anticipated that this could be accomplished by forming new units. For instance, ten new companies of military police would be added between 2002 and 2007, with a total compliment of 1800 personnel.

In summary, "the Army National Guard has realigned its force structure somewhat to face the new demands of the war on terror. For the future, most indications point toward the Guard slowly assuming homeland security as one of its primary roles, of roughly equal emphasis with additional war-fighting forces for conflicts abroad."[11]

In keeping with this restructuring, Marine Corps General Charles Kulak coined the phrase *a three-block war*. This was meant to embrace the spectrum of operations: from humanitarian missions, through peacekeeping and peace enforcement actions, to full-blown combat—possibly within the area of three blocks. In order to succeed, the force deployed must be

---

11. Ibid., 1.

able to effectively make the transition from one phase to another, while accenting its peace associated responsibilities.

The area of operations between peacekeeping and peace enforcement is well described as *the gray zone*. There being no neat division that allows for precise application. While some are seen as especially gifted in negotiating such situations.

Former President Bush was correct when he announced that the major combat operations in Iraq were concluded. He was also accurate in anticipating additional loss of life in pursuit of an extended peace. Those who supposed that the end of major combat operations precluded substantial casualties were unfortunately not accurate.

Nor was the issue precisely the same as when it was decided to wage a preemptive conflict. So that one had to weigh the consequences of withdrawing too hastily or continue beyond a preferable time for disengagement. Matters can appear differently in retrospect, so that our memories of former times are suspect.

American international policy reveals a combination of humanitarian concern and national interests. These jostle around for favorable consideration. Consequently, we ought not assume that what we perceive as in our national interests is necessarily compatible with what is good for other nation states. Consequently, there is justification for thinking in terms of a global community.

In any case, 9/11 has greatly altered the way we perceive life. Nor is there a prospect of returning to former ways. Consequently, life is in greater jeopardy. Calling for greater diligence and realistic expectations. In the memorable lyrics of Charles Wesley, "To serve this present age, my calling to fulfil; O may it all my powers engage, to do my Master's will."

Liberty

BORN FREE! HOW THOROUGHLY inviting! Although hard to imagine for hose experiencing life from the interim between paradise lost and regained.

Free to experience God's edifying presence. Free to enjoy life together. Free to be engaged in meaningful activity. Born free!

As such, endowed by our Creator. Inciting the psalmist to reflect: "When I consider your heavens, the work of your fingers, the moon and the stars, which you have set in place, what is man that you are mindful of him? You made him a little lower than the heavenly beings, and crowned him with glory and honor. You made him ruler over the works of your hands" (Psa. 8:3–6).

In Jewish terms, man was free to serve his inclination to do good. Not as yet inhibited by his eventual bad inclination. Nor experientially aware of what would be involved in the transformation. In what might be described as a state of blessed innocence, analogous to that of a child.

Genuine freedom requires a reality check. We assuredly live in God's world by means of his grace. Otherwise, our perception of freedom is distorted. We attempt to usurp divine prerogatives—as with humanism, while not uncommonly abiding by the code of the survival of those most fit. Or as my maternal grandmother would on occasion observe, "Each on his own, and the devil get the hindmost."

Ejected from paradise, man faced a much less inviting future. While not the best, it was not the worst of situations. In that God had not forsaken his wayward creatures. In proverbial terms, there was a light at the end of the tunnel.

Now Cain chose for the worse, while his sibling Abel, opted for the better. As for the former, he offered a token sacrifice, while the latter presented a prized portion from the firstborn of his flock. Consequently, God was pleased with Abel's offering, but displeased with that of Cain. Leading to the tragic results detailed in another context.

Individual choices can build toward a consensus. As was the case at the time of Noah, when the Lord observed how great man's wickedness had become, since "every inclination of the thoughts of his heart was only evil all the time" (Gen. 6:5). So that God brought the great flood, as if to cleanse the world from its contagion, and allow for a better alternative with the descendants of righteous Noah.

Nevertheless, the evil inclination continued to dominate. As evidenced by the erection of the tower of Babel. As a pretentious monument to human ingenuity. While quite without deference to God. Resulting in the dispersion of the people, less their degradation be further exploited.

God's initiative took a more positive turn with the call of Abraham. As previously noted, he instructed the patriarch: "leave your country, your people and your father's household and go to the land I will show you" (Gen. 12:1). Along with the promise that the Lord would make him into a great nation, enhance his reputation, make him a blessing, bless those who blessed him and curse those who cursed him, resulting in the blessing of all peoples.

So the Patriarch took his leave. It was his choice, and he chose wisely. "Abram believed the Lord, and it was counted to him as righteousness" (Gen. 15:6). Here the emphasis is not on what the patriarch did, but his motivation for doing so. Accordingly, his confidence in God's promise.

Now Jacob showed favoritism for his youngest son Joseph. Inciting his siblings to hatred. So that they sold him into bondage. "The Lord was with Joseph and he prospered" (Gen. 39:2). Initially, and in spite of adverse developments, so that he informed his brothers: "But God sent me ahead of you to preserve for you a remnant on earth and to save your lives by a great deliverance" (Gen. 45:7).

For the time being, the Israelites found refuge in Egypt. But things took a decided turn for the worse with a subsequent ruler, who no longer looked with favor on them. Instead, he subjected them to forced and unrelenting labor. So that they cried out to the Lord for deliverance. This was described in Jewish tradition as the *seventh falling away*, at a time when human depravity reached its worst.

The Divine Mandates

Likewise, a time when the Israelites were deprived of their freedom. As inhumane treatment. Recalled as such by successive generations.

God heard the cry of his people, and brought about their deliverance. They were freed to covenant with him in the wilderness. Then to pursue their calling as the chosen people, as a light to the Gentiles.

When it came time to renew their covenant with the Almighty Joshua enjoined the people: "Now fear the Lord and serve him with all faithfulness. But if serving the Lord seems undesirable to you, then choose for yourselves this day whom you will serve. But as for me and my household, we will serve the Lord" (Josh. 24:14–15).

Soliciting the response of the people, "Far be it from us to forsake the Lord to serve other gods!" Since it was he who delivered them from bondage, sustained them during their wilderness wandering, and settled them in the promised land.

Joshua then protested, "You are not able to serve the Lord." Not without his enablement. And not without falling tragically short.

But the people insisted, "We will serve the Lord our God and obey him." So that Joshua compiled instructions for them, so that they might pursue their righteous intent. His misgivings aside.

The resolve of the people vacillated with the volatile time of the judges. As previously allowed, they would succumb to their sinful ways. Unable to control the enemy within, they fell prey to the enemy without. At which, they cried out to the Lord in their distress. Once delivered, they enjoyed a time of relative peace. Only to again fall into temptation, resulting in oppression.

The monarchy brought a more pronounced semblance of order than revealed in the days of the judges. As noted earlier, it consisted of a system of checks and balances. Involving the ruler, school of the prophets, priestly establishment, wisdom tradition, and not to be overlooked—the general populace. Consequently, a concert of wills negotiated the way set before them.

The exile further restricted the freedom of the chosen people. Those carried away into a foreign environ were faced with the dilemma of how to maintain their convictions while making reasonable accommodations. Such as Daniel and his companions. Those left behind had to struggle with chaotic conditions.

Liberty

With their return from exile, the Israelites had to cope with hostile inhabitants. In the face of difficult obstacles, they persisted in their endeavor. As a result, they would achieve a limited success.

As touched on earlier, the era between the testaments received mixed reviews. Some welcomed the opportunity to cast aside the remains of a no longer treasured tradition. Thus easing the reproach of their pagan neighbors. Others felt forsaken with the demise of the school of the prophets.

Their Messianic hope survived the ordeal. Recalling the sage observation, "The Lord is slow in keeping his promises, as some understand slowness. He is patient with you, not wanting anyone to perish, but everyone to come to repentance" (2 Pet. 3:9). Suggesting that he opts for the most opportune time to bring to pass his gracious purposes. Even though persons would speed up the process, with less to show for it.

The specific features of the Messianic time table are more difficult to determine. The return of the chosen people to the promised land appears to have put one piece in place. The Hellenic culture and language provided a common link. The expanse and favorable conditions associated with the Roman Empire likewise seem conducive. Areas once difficult to penetrate now provided a ready access.

Then there was the availability of an assortment of individuals. Like Mary, who allowed: "I am the Lord's servant. May it be to me as you have said (Luke 1:38). Such as Simeon, who "was waiting or the consolation of Israel" (Luke 2:25). As with John the Baptist, who quoted from the prophet Isaiah: "Prepare the way for the Lord, make straight paths for him" (Luke 3:4; Isa. 40:3). Most conspicuously with Jesus, who agonizingly prayed: "Father, if you are willing, take this cup from me; yet not my will but yours be done" (Luke 22:42). Each exercising the freedom with which they had been endowed.

As again noted, Jesus declared: "So if the Son sets you free, you will be free indeed" (John 8:36). Free indeed, since some who are said to be free are in spiritual bondage. While some who are slaves are promised spiritual deliverance.

This serves as an earnest of things yet to come. "Behold, I am coming soon!" the risen and ascended Lord exclaims. "Blessed is he who keeps the words of the prophecy in this book" (Rev. 22:7).

"The Spirit and the bride (with reference to the church) say, 'Come!' And let him who hears (without exception) say, 'Come!' Whoever is thirsty, let him come, and whoever wishes, let him take the free gift of the water of life."

"Amen," the compliant author enthusiastically responds. "Come, Lord Jesus." Having been granted the freedom of choice, and wisely exercised it. While enduring persecution, in quest for the celestial city. His liberty greatly enhanced by a rigorous engagement in service.

It remains to touch on several relevant essays concerning the exercise of freedom. Morris Chapman observes, "We can't manufacture renewal. It is not something we can work to achieve. It is something for which we must pray."[1] Initially endowed with freedom by the Creator, we cannot expect to enhance it without his involvement. As observed by the sage, "First things first."

"Prayer must underwrite everything we accomplish in this nation," continues Chapman (p. 12). Major undertakings and minor considerations. Calling for a prayer alert. With the intent to establish a relentless prayer chain.

"There is much right with this country," he continues. "There is little doubt about it. I am always glad to come home to these United State of America" (p. 13). Recalling a time when I had returned from a short term teaching assignment in Nigeria. At the airline check-out the attendant greeted me: "Welcome home." I was virtually moved to tears. "However, that does not mean that we are never in need of a house cleaning when we come home. Things get dusty, sometimes downright dirty."

In brief, America is desperately I need of a spiritual awakening. Such as has occurred on occasion in the past. Lest its vitality continue to diminish. Sinking increasingly into an inept conglomeration.

"We have not had a national revival in this country for over 85 years," Chapman recalls. "It was the aftermath of the Welsh revival, which began, in my understanding, one night when a young girl in a small church in the midst of a testimonial meeting stood up to say, 'I love the Lord Jesus Christ with all my heart.' So simple as to be profound. Stirred by the Holy Spirit of God, the congregation was electrified."

"Repentance came to the hearts of the people. They were kneeling at the altar, praying, some coming to know Christ as Savior, and others renewing their covenant with God. Revival swept from church to church and across that nation and came to America." As a welcomed visitation.

Some doubted its integrity. Thinking that the resolve of those implicated would soon diminish. Their doubts were in measure justified, since it

---

1. Chapman, "Kneel Down and Be Counted," 11.

was estimated that within five years only 80 % of those who had responded still continued in their resolve.

"The African antelope called the gnu has an interesting characteristic. When attacked, the gnu kneels and returns the attack from its knees. That is a great lesson for all of us. We can only overcome those who hinder the work of God by going to God in prayer. Unless we do, there is no power, no driving force" (p. 15).

"What hope is there? Is it too late to change course and preserve the freedoms we have cherished in this greatest nation on earth? There is a way, and that way is the way of faith by conviction" (p. 18). Recalling the saying, "With God there is hope; without God there is none.

"A person of faith does not waste time on indecision. Neither did Daniel or his friends. They didn't hold a stockholder's meeting to decide what to do. They already, by faith, knew and understood God's purposes. There is nothing to lose and everything to gain by faith."

"So, we are to kneel down and be counted. We are to stand tall on our knees. Yes, we are to stand, but when we stand we must know we have been with God. Before we talk to others about God we need to talk to God about them. We need to pray for those who would oppose the truth of God's Holy Word."

Chapman recalls the pertinent comments of a Romanian pastor: "We thought that if today there is freedom that is taken away from us, if tomorrow another freedom is taken away from us, if the next day they will close a church and the day after they will put in prison one of our very great Christian leaders, it will be all right. We still had something to eat. But when we ended up in bondage, we had nothing" (p. 20).

"And there is only one way out of bondage—celebration and sacrifice." Celebration of that with which we are endowed. Sacrifice so as to preserve it, as a legacy for subsequent generations.

"The politicians do not have the ultimate answer for the economy, morality, or ethics. The answer comes by faith. We need to pray for the leaders of our land that the spirit of God would stir us and them for His glory. We need a stirring. We need revival. We need a spiritual awakening" (p. 21). Only then can we approximate our God-given potential as individuals and as a nation.

Lynn Buzzard insists in a second essay: "It is crucial that we understand the context in which the constitutional issues of church and state are fought today. The context is one of enormous moral and spiritual crisis in this county."[2] "We don't need scholars to tell us about some of these crises because we see them in our homes, our children, and all sorts of statistics."

"Discussions about church and state are non longer merely a domestic issue. While Russians seek new spiritual values, enormous secularizing forces continue to sweep through societies such as ours" (p. 33). "Amid all of these cultural and worldwide concerns and changes swirling around us, the phrase *the wall of separation* has become a pivotal point of discussion." Although the expression is not found in the Constitution, nor does it have any judicial sanction.

Nevertheless, it has some redeeming features. Such as the means whereby government is prohibited from establishing one religion, to the exclusion of others. Or when it demand conformity to a political policy offensive to a religious community.

"A second area in which the image is appropriate occurs where we see the political use of religion. There will always be a temptation on the part of any political faction or political forces to attempt to align themselves with some religious group in order to get their publicity and support" (pp. 34–35). It has happened in the past, and no doubt will occur again in the future.

"A third area involves the dangers created by the increasingly regulatory state. The problem in the United States is primarily not a problem of overt oppression. The most serious problems are the realities of expanding and regulatory state and federal governments that squeeze religion out on piecemeal basis" (p. 35). While justified as *public policy* and/or *compelling state interest*. "The regulatory state can be just as destructive to the distinctive of religious faith as can a hostile state. In fact, it can be worse, because the hostile state must be open about it, and it invites prophetic response and perhaps even civil disobedience."

"The state which is out to do us 'good' is the most dangerous state. It deludes itself about its real, ultimate purposes. This type of state invites us to recognize the importance of the Free Exercise Clause. In one sense, the Free Exercise Clause is now the most critical protection that the church has." To what extent will it "provide some protection, particularly for dissenter traditions which emphasize special perspectives and values and want to be different?"

This protection was seriously compromised by the *Employment Division v. Smith* Supreme Court ruling. Since the court ruled that the

---

2. Buzzard, "Separation of Church, State, and Religious Liberty," 32.

government need no longer establish a compelling state interest need be required to intrude on sincerely held religious beliefs. "It means that the Court will now not be a protector of religious liberty because the state almost never will set out deliberately to target religion. It will almost always be in the context of a supposedly neutral regulation" (p. 36).

Buzzard quotes Mark DeWolf Howe as saying, "The Supreme Court has a right to make history but not to rewrite it." "History is clear that men of the original 13 states had established churches and many other forms of preference for religion, including particular religions, and that the framers of the constitution had no intention of creating a modern secular state" (P. 37).

"There is a tendency of people who use the slogan to try to view the framers through today's filters that project onto them our current definitions rather than the definitions by which they lived." Not uncommonly promoting what they graphically describe as *a living constitution*. One said to keep pace with the changing times, but out of touch with our founding fathers.

"A further way in which the image of separation of church and state distorts proper policy is by encouraging, by its very language, a 'separation' of life into different spheres" (p. 38). Namely, the sacred and the secular. "Such a separation of life into that kind of rigid compartmentalization is both impossible and undesirable."

"Indeed, any attempt to suggest that you can have a neutral public square is similarly doomed to failure. There is no such thing as a neutral government" (p. 39). Some supposed values exist, whether we recognize them or not.

"Only now are we beginning to recover the urgency of some of these issues and reject this sort of schizophrenia which infected us. In fact, the public affairs were deeply shaped by Christian cultural values. That's no longer true. The world has radically changed" (p. 41). Threatening to undermine the values which have brought into being and sustained our nation.

Consider, for instance, our public school policy. "No one would doubt that a public school as part of an exploration of issues of sexuality might invite a representative of Planned Parenthood to talk about his or her views." But should one be invited to speak concerning a Christian perspective on sexuality, "immediately many organizations would raise the separation-of-church-and-state banner and insist this was impermissible intrusion. Any idea which is religious or even linked to religion, such as a moral idea with religious heritage, is now suspect."

The Divine Mandates

"The sad reality of this erroneous perspective is that it is held by many devout Christians" (p. 42). Who fail to see its implications. Or have compartmentalized their faith. While notably lacking a Christian world view.

What is to be done? "First, we need to reexamine our images and models" (p. 43). So as to creatively interact with our culture. Without compromising prized convictions.

"Second, we need to develop a serious theological conversation about jurisprudence and the state. Such a conversation must be biblically sound, integrative of different disciplines, and able to cite relevant authorities."

"Third, we need to reject openly and candidly the notion that absolutes and moral values must be held privately but not discussed publicly. To talk about absolutes and moral values is not to diminish liberty, but, in fact, to give liberty character and focus" (p. 44). The quest for truth requires courage.

"Fourth, we have to recover our prophetic stance, then we have to refuse to be co-opted. We have to refuse to succumb to the lure of being included with all the other important people." As regards the example of the prophet, he "is human, yet he employs notes one octave too high for our ears. He experiences moments that defy our understanding. He is neither 'a singing saint' nor a 'moralizing poet,' but an assaulter of the mind. Often his words begin to burn where conscience ends."[3]

"Finally, we need to remember in all of this what is at risk. Issues of religious liberty and freedom are not simply questions of a free church. Liberty must always be linked to moral and spiritual values" (p. 45). Consequently, "the whole question of moral and spiritual values in the role of religion is not just a question of the freedom of the church to do its thing. The question is what kind of culture and what kind of society are we going to have in which to rear our children?" Amen.

Carl F. H. Henry cogently observes in yet another study, "To coerce belief has not value either to God or humans who are forced to comply against their will."[4] It is of no value to God since it is quite lacking in devotion. It is of no value to humans in that it requires no righteous resolve as a impetus to moral behavior.

The most basic of all human liberties is religious liberty," Henry continues. "The choice one makes between the rival gods bears significantly on the definition of justice and human duties and rights." In greater detail,

---

3. Heschel, *The Prophets*, 10.
4. Henry, "Religious Liberty As a Cause Celebre," 65.

Liberty

"While justice is a critical component of corporate life, its meaning is variously understood. This not uncommonly leads to confusion, incrimination, and even conflict."[5]

"The modern secular state distorts the Protestant Reformation's emphasis on freedom to worship God in accord with a good conscience, into the right of unqualified freedom from God and from religion. Yet religious liberty as a formal civic right embraces even the freedom to espouse atheism. If religious freedom is a fundamental right, it belongs to all" (pp. 65–66).

"Atheism now often takes the form of a pseudo-religion. Secular humanism manipulates the term *religion* to its own advantage. It holds that religion is conceptually false whenever it designates an objectively existing divinity, while it claims at time to be itself a religion" (p. 66). When human values, however defined, are alleged to be of ultimate concern.

While a generation ago Jews may have faced the severest persecution, "Christians are at present the main objects of discrimination and persecution. This is, in part, due to the global missionary presence of Christianity. Hostility is invited also by the blow to Islamic pride posed by the technologically superior West, which Islam views as formally Christian."

"In view of the lifting of restrictions on Christianity by Soviet sphere nations, the repressive treatment of Christian minorities by Islamic nations and Communist mainland China becomes glaringly conspicuous. The situation in Turkey and Egypt is far from desirable, but that in Saudi Arabia is more deplorable" (p. 67). "Saudi Arabia not only refuses to approve basic religious liberties, but it also withholds from Christians even the *dhimma*, or protection, of the ongoing practice of Christianity."

Discussion of *a new world order* is meaningless "unless the basic right of religious freedom is addressed in all nations of the world." Not simply in select instances, as a partisan concern. While addressing bondage in its multi-faceted form. As in the case of involuntary prostitution.

"A government policy that aims mostly to preserve a delicate balance of political interests while it escapes dialogue at the deeper level of human duties and rights has only transitory pragmatic value," Henry cautions. "Any nation that professes profound dedication to human rights cannot without penalty forever postpone interaction over the most fundamental of all rights, namely, religious liberty" (p. 71).

---

5. Inch, *The Enigma of Justice*, p. vii.

The Divine Mandates

Religious liberty is an urgent concern. "Despite the pride of the West in the technological achievements of modernity, religious intolerance and persecution remain besetting evils of much of the contemporary world. The once dominantly Christian West is now sinking into unbridled naturalism, and an atheistic world view often accommodates tyrannical government and a disdain for religion." In the United States, "the constitutional assurance of free religious expression is increasingly subordinated to as exaggerated and distorted emphasis on religious nonestablishment" (p. 73).

"In fulfilling her world mission, the church faces the possibility of two costly misjudgments, both of which can only gratify Satan and his minions. The first danger, to which ecumenical Christianity succumbed, is a dilution of its message into a politico-economic cultural concentration that ignores the biblical gospel of personal regeneration" (p. 74). A social engagement void of compelling spiritual convictions to sustain it.

"The second danger is the evangelical concentration on personal evangelism that withdraws from cultural concerns and permits alien forces to shape the public area, so that the church is marginalized and functions in society only by the tolerance of her foes" (pp. 74–75). As if having taken a leave of absence from one's social accountability.

"The Western world is unfortunately trapped in a costly compromise of its own spiritual heritage. To be sure, it champions compatible social values such as political self-determination, private property, capitalism, and human rights." On the other hand, "It eclipses the doctrine of divine judgement, even of divine creation, of sin and redemption, and of the regenerate church as a new society" (p. 76). Seizing on the notion of social mandates, without their divine impetus.

"Secular humanism exploits this vacuum and projects illusory utopias." In greater detail, "In the place of the old attitudes involved in worship and prayer the humanist finds his religious emotions expressed in a heightened sense of personal life and in a cooperative effort to promote social well-being."[6]

"If in the present world a bold insistence on religious liberty is to arise as never before, it is the 35 million adult, born-again Christians in America who ought not to take the lead by way of gratitude for their own inheritance and experience. Losing God is what we have most to fear. If we love Him we shall inevitably lose the culture also, and ourselves as well" (p. 77). Along

---

6. *Humanist Manifest 1*, Eighth affirmation.

with losing God, we lose the notion of divine mandates, that concerning liberty in particular.

All of which recalls an excerpt from *The Universal Declaration of Human Rights,* "Everyone has the right of freedom of thought, conscience and religion; this right includes freedom to change his religion or belief, and freedom, either alone or in community with others and in public or private, to manifest his religion or belief in teaching, practice, worship and observance."[7] Would that this were true!

---

7. *The Universal Declaration of Human Rights,* Article 18.

Pursuit of Happiness

Happiness ranges from contentment to intense joy. Even so, there is little precise correlation between circumstances and our response to them. So that some are content with little, while others are dissatisfied with much. In fact, the more we have, the more we seem to want.

Happiness may emerge from a variety of pleasant experiences. Such as when watching a sunset, enjoying a tasty meal, or animated discussion. Sometimes as a result of a long awaited vacation. Sometimes when quite unexpected.

We are not endowed with happiness per se, but its *pursuit*. Which would suggest that happiness can be allusive, fleeting, and transitory. Resulting in part from various conditions that are implicated. Such as that which pertains to our health, companions, or whether there are distractions.

The term *blessed* serves as a near equivalent. However, the accent seems to be more on the actual situation than one's subjective perception of it. As aptly observe d, "Appearances can be deceiving."

In greater detail, "Blessed is the man who finds wisdom, the man who gains understanding, for she is more profitable than silver and yields better returns than gold" (Prov. 3:13–14). "Just as the artisan forges his sword or weaves a rug, so the sage tells us how to live life with finesse. He corrects those of us who blunder along, from one day to the next, saying the wrong thing, doing the wrong thing, wishing we could do better."[1]

Which bring to mind the cast in wisdom literature. The *wise* welcomes instruction; with understanding, gains insight; with insight, skill in living;

---

1. Inch, *Understanding Bible Prophecy*, 70.

with skill, the ability to plan ahead; with all, to cultivate a righteous life. In keeping with God's gracious purposes.

Conversely, the *fool* resists instruction; otherwise put, is obstinate; as the saying goes: "resembles an accident waiting to happen." As such, a menace to self and one's associates. Thus involving God's deserving displeasure.

The *scoffer* is not wise, but more resembles the fool. Not only does he or she dislike correction, but holds the truth up to ridicule. Such are a plague for those with good intentions.

The *sluggard* is reluctant to engage in constructive activity. If initiated, he or she is reticent to carry it through to a successful conclusion. Such are also reluctant to face up to pressing issues. And may be characterized from time to time as restless, helpless, useless, and exasperating.

A *friend* loves at all times, and a brother is born for adversity" (Prov. 17:17). Fair weather or the converse. A friend is also candid, accepting, reassuring, and tactful. In consort with one's brother.

The *simple person* is as yet uninformed. Such are in need of a worthy mentor. Otherwise, they will continue to flounder. They appear to be many in number.

Some prominent features of wisdom literature are as follows: (1) as a reality check, (2) a point of contact, (3) an emphasis on practical living, (4) a call to embrace God's world, (5) an impetus to creativity, (6) a cause for humility, (7) a return to basics, (8) a commentary on creation, (9) hence an appeal to general revelation, (10) as such in anticipation of special revelation, (11) an appreciation of one's heritage, (12) often expressed in poetic fashion, (13) as a means of encouragement, (14) conversely, an occasion for warning, (15) with accent on life and vigor, (16) not to the exclusion of illness and demise (17) an esteem for maturity, (18) a sense of propriety, (19), a rebuke to privilege, (20) a call to reflection, and (21) a summons to worship. All things considered, a means of blessing.

Turning to another text, "He who despises his neighbor sins, but blessed is he who is kind to the needy" (Prov 14:21). On one occasion, a certain *expert in the law* inquired of Jesus: "Teacher, what must I do to inherit eternal life?" (Luke 10:25). He may simply have been interested in Jesus' perception, rather than seeking to discredit him.

In characteristic fashion, Jesus answers a question with a question. "What is written in the Law? How do you read it?

The inquirer answered: "'Love the Lord your God with all your heart and with all your will and with all your strength, with all your mind'; and 'Love your neighbor as yourself.'"

"You have answered correctly." Jesus commended him. "Do this and you shall live." "Of course, it is one thing to interpret the law correctly, another to internalize and perform it. Returning to the lawyer's original question concerning behavior appropriate to eternal life, then, Jesus counsels not only this representation of the law but also its practice."[2]

But he wanting to justify himself, inquired further: "And who is my neighbor?" He was perhaps thinking of the Gentiles, and what obligations he had in this regard. In any case, as a means of justifying his misgivings.

In reply, Jesus told a parable concerning a man who fell into the hands of thieves, who stripped him of his clothes, beat him and went away, leaving him half dead." A priest happened to come along, but when he saw the injured man, pointedly passed by on the opposite side of the road. He perhaps feared for his own life, or otherwise justified his indifference. A Levite subsequently came along, and he too passed by on *the other side.* Likewise unavailable.

In contrast, a Samaritan approached the place where the man lay, and when he saw him, he went and bandaged his wounds. Then he put the man on his donkey, took him to an inn, and took care of him. The next day, he gave two silver coins to the inn-keeper, along with the instruction to look after him, "and when I return, I will reimburse you for any extra expense you may have."

Which of these three do you think was a neighbor to the man who fell into the hands of robbers?" he then inquired.

"The one who had mercy on him," the expert in the law allowed. We are thus alerted to the fact that one's neighbor is not one who acts in neighborly fashion toward us, but depends on our behavior toward him or her. Which allows for no exceptions.

Jesus then admonished him, "Go and do likewise." And in doing so, he would be greatly blessed.

Considering yet another text, "Whoever gives heed to instruction prospers, and blessed is he who trusts in the Lord" (Prov. 16:20). Initially, one must *hear* what is said. This involves comprehension. Involving the context, perspective, and application. As for *context*, there is both its larger

---

2. Green, *The Gospel of Luke*, 428.

and more immediate setting. The former tuning into the divine agenda, while the latter focuses on the specific situation.

As concerns *perspective*, one must attempt to view the issue from a perspective other than his or her own. This is assuredly the case when involving divine instruction, and in a more qualified sense to that of a sage. Such is likewise involved in genuine dialogue, which embraces differing points of view.

With regard to *application*, what does love entail? Perhaps sharing with someone who is poverty stricken. Perhaps being patient with the spiritual progress of an associate. Perhaps involving personal risk. Every situation is in some way unique, calling for a creative response.

Having heard, one must *heed*. Learn in order to do. Not simply to store knowledge away, as a form of materialism.

Acquire skill for the purpose of putting it to good use. As would an artisan. Recalling a time when I joined others watching a Hebron potter apply his trade. There were murmurs of appreciation as the vessel began to take shape. When finished, it was a work to be admired.

By all means, trust in the Lord. When Fanny Crosby was only six weeks old, she lost her sight because of a doctor's error. "I have always believed," she allowed, "that the good Lord, in His infinite mercy, by this means consecrated me to the work that I am still permitted to do."[3] As a result of her trust and endeavor, generations have been greatly blessed by her in inspiring hymns.

"All the way my Savior leads me," she confides. "What have I to ask beside? Can I doubt His tender mercy, who through life has been my guide?" Thus blessed, and providing a blessing to others.

The sage also reminds us, "Where there is no revelation, the people cast off restraint; but blessed is he who keeps the law" (Prov. 29:18)/ *Revelation* means to disclose that which was previously unknown. For instance, there is *general revelation*: "For since the creation of the world God's invisible qualities—his eternal power and divine nature—have been clearly seen, being understood from what has been made, so that men are without excuse" (Rom. 1:20).

"How universal is this perception? The flow of Paul's argument makes any limitation impossible. Those who perceive the attributes of

---

3. *The One Year Book of Hymns*, January 16.

God in creation must be the same as those who suppress the truth in unrighteousness."[4]

What does this perception entail? His inherent capability, as evidenced the creation of the universe—in its entirety, particulars, and how they coalesce. Likewise, concerning his benevolent character. Thus given to generously sharing his bounty with others.

Moreover, "For prophecy never had its origin in the will of man, but men spoke from God as they were carried along by the Holy Spirit" (2 Peter 1:21). Thus constituting *special revelation*, imparting knowledge concerning God's redemptive initiative. Consequently, blessed are those who abide by their covenant obligations.

A final word from the sage, "The memory of the righteous will be a blessing, but the name of the wicked will not" (Prov. 10:7). Yes, memories can be a blessing or not. For instance, my mother was past the age when women usually give birth and in poor health when I was conceived. Even so, I doubt that she ever gave serious thought to having an abortion. So that I am indebted to her for life, and the opportunity to engage in service. Blessed memory!

My devoted wife Joan, served in a parental role to many of our students who studied overseas with us. In this capacity, offering counsel and encouragement. While otherwise engaged in the work of the institute. Blessed memory!

Not so in other instances. Like that of a bully who delighted in making life miserable for my childhood friends and me. So that I felt obligated to look out for the welfare of some of those more vulnerable. A memory better forgotten!

Now when Jesus saw the multitude, "he went up on a mountainside and sat down. His disciples approached him and he began to teach them" (Matt. 5:1–2). Jesus, his disciples, and the multitude. Jesus is featured as their mentor. He embodies the way of the righteous (cr. Psa. 1:1–3).

His disciples had until recently been indistinguishable from the multitude. Now they stood apart from the rest. They could not grasp what this would involve. And they would continue to struggle with its significance.

The multitude sensed that their lives had been altered. It was not something that they could readily grasp, except as it was associated with Jesus. Consequently, they stared at each other across a divide that would be accentuated in eternity.

---

4. Moo, *The Epistle to the Romans*, 105.

Blessed are the poor in spirit, for theirs is the kingdom of heaven," Jesus declared. "In Hebrew parlance the 'poor' were not simply the economically disadvantaged but those who in their need had turned to God for help."[5] Poverty as such was not thought desirable or approved.

Such blessing is available to those who realize their need. And in doing so, petition the Lord to meet that need. Thus turning from their wicked ways.

Is this to say that there can be no pleasure in evil behavior? No, although its euphoric effect soon wears off. Often plagued by relentless feelings of guilt. If not, then set in their evil ways.

Conversely, the blessing of which Jesus speaks serves as an earnest of things to come. Happiness now, and greater happiness in the future. Giving rise to the sage encouragement, "The best is yet to come."

Blessed are those who mourn, for they will be comforted." That is, those who are overwhelmed with their own waywardness, and the evil so prevalent in the world. So that they are moved to tears, repentance, and intercession.

Such will be comforted. In their present duress. Even more so as salvation history unfolds. In terms of the hymn lyrics, "When the saints go marching in." Lord, I want to be in the blessed company, when the saints go marching in.

As set over against those who are relatively content with that which offends God. Such as are willing to let evil triumph. Providing, that is, that meanwhile they can be entertained.

"Blessed are the meek, for they will inherit the earth." Such as are not obsessed with the quest for importance. Conversely, happily accepting the opportunities that life affords. As for the former, it proves to be a never ending struggle. With countless frustrations along the way.

As for the latter, it anticipates pleasant surprises. Expressions of gratitude, delightful experiences, and inviting situations. While confident that the Lord will supply all that is genuinely needed. Leading to lasting gratification.

"Blessed are those who hunger and thirst for righteousness, for they will be filled." The imagery is largely lost on those accustomed to having food and drink readily available. I recall only one extended time when unable to satisfy my hunger. It was when serving in the military overseas, and awaiting deployment. Even then, we had enough to sustain life.

5. Mounce, *Matthew*, 38.

Some tragically feel driven to the use of drugs. So much so that they will steal in order to sustain their habit. In contrast, righteousness is an inviting prospect. One that is eminently worthy of our endeavor. Since we were meant to experience the presence of the Lord, nothing else will actually satisfy.

"Blessed are the merciful, for they will be shown mercy." *Mercy* is an expression of love that takes into consideration the frailty of another. In this regard, C. S. Lewis observed that because God loves us, he attempts to make us lovable. Thus preserving justice in the process.

In this regard, Jesus admonished: "Be merciful, just as your Father is merciful" (Luke 6:36). Consequently, the exercise of mercy is an eloquent expression of the divine nature. One holds out great promise, but in this life and that to come.

"Blessed are the pure in heart, for they will see God." Those who are not agitated by the struggle between the good and evil inclinations. Instead. They are focused on fulfilling God's purpose for their lives. Cultivated by love, now motivated by love.

"In Revelation the blessed 'will see his face' (Rev. 22:4). Although the promise is primarily eschatological, it can also be realized in a spiritual sense at the present time. Genuine purity provides an immediate and profound experience of the presence and power of God."[6]

"Blessed are the peacemakers, for they will be called sons of God." In Jewish tradition, it is said that such are children of the world to come. When meaningful relationships prevail, and discord vanishes. When life is no longer complicated by the presence of evil.

This implies active engagement rather than passive retreat. Since all that is necessary for evil to triumph is for good persons to do nothing. Conversely, peacemaking is something. Ranging from persuasion to more restrictive behavior. Calling for careful deliberation, resolute action, and cooperative endeavor. And greatly enhanced by spiritual maturity.

"Blessed are those who are persecuted because of righteousness, for theirs is the kingdom of heaven." In fact, everyone who wants to live a godly life in Christ Jesus will be persecuted while evil men and impostors will go from bad to worse, deceiving and being deceived" (2 Tim. 3:12–13). In some measure, although martyrdom is reserved for a relatively few.

While in contrast to evil persons and those who pretend to be what they are not. Since they accommodate to the prevailing culture surrounding

---

6. Ibid., 41.

them. Choosing the ways of men rather than the more rigorous way of God. Consequently, not to be emulated.

In greater detail, "Blessed are you when people insult you, persecute you and falsely say all kinds of evil against you because of me. Rejoice and be glad, because great is your reward in heaven, for in the same way they persecuted the prophets who were before you." And even now such are blessed, as an earnest of things to come.

It was with this in mind that I previously explored *Whispers of Heaven* as a harbinger of things to come.[7] Which provides the excerpts that follow. These speak for themselves.

Mt. Katahdin affords many memories. Most are good. Some are genuinely exhilarating.

If one takes the Hunt Trail, it is 5.2 miles from the foot of Mt. Katahdin to its peak. Persons characteristically begin the climb at the crack of dawn. The path from the camp ground winds through dense foliage. One can see only to the turn ahead.

There are sounds native to the forest. They bear little similarity to those that accompany urban living. Most pronounced is that of water cascading over rocks. It continues to build in volume.

Before long we can make out a stream through the trees. It seems intent on reaching its destination. Eventually, we come to a crude bridge spanning a narrow gorge. After crossing over, the incline increases.

Some time later, we approach the tree line. Scrub trees replace their towering cousins. Off to one side is an alternative ridge. From a vantage point we can look back to the valley below. Soon there are no trees to block our view. Slopes appear on both sides as the tree line continues to recede.

Still, our purview is limited. We can see only to the top of the next rise. When we have reached it, another beckons us from the distance. I would not want it otherwise, since the challenge is quite sufficient for the present. Too much too soon would be discouraging.

With one final effort, we stand erect—greeting by a breathtaking view. The slopes plunge headlong into the tree line, giving the impression of a majestic monument to God's ingenuity. Her and there we can make out a pond decorating the landscape. Beyond, in the distance, is the horizon.

The clouds seem to hand low. At times you feel as if you could touch them. The air seems fresher and more invigorating. Life takes on a new lease.

---

7. Inch, *Whispers of Heaven & Heaven According to Matthew*, 11–14.

It helps to have climbed with others. Good things are best shared. A companion grins at you. He does not have to say anything; the grin says it all.

Our attention is diverted. The sun peaks out from behind a cloud, casting shadows across the landscape. It creeps up the slopes, accentuating one feature after another. It sparkles in the water below.

I imagine this is what heaven will be like, only better. It will have been a difficult climb, but well worth it. We will have bonded with others on the way, with God and our fellow pilgrims. Sometimes we were tempted to turn back, but now glad that we did not do so.

What of those who did not make the effort? They will never know what heaven is like. One feels sorry for them.

* * *

World War II lyrics come to mind: "Gonna take a sentimental journey, gonna set my mind at ease. Gonna take a sentimental journey, to renew old memories." I left for military service the day after my eighteenth birthday. My mother and a family friend drove me to the station, where I along with others boarded a train headed for the uncertainties that awaited us.

I did get home on leave occasionally. Most vivid in my recollection was the time I returned from overseas. As the train approached my village, I could make out familiar landmarks. I experienced a warm, fuzzy feeling within. Indeed, it was a sentimental journey home.

Stepping off the train, I headed for my father's store. He was turned toward the shelves, so that he did not see me enter. I leaned across the counter, my head on a level with his, waiting for him to turn around. When he did, a shocked expression crossed his face. It was not what I had intended. Upon recovering, he welcomed me home.

After that, I crossed the road to our home where my mother awaited me. A friend had seen me get off the train, and ran to alert her. She threw her arms around me as she had done countless times previously. This time she wept tears of joy.

The old family house still stands, although in disrepair. Mother died some years ago, and Dad several years later. My siblings have likewise passed away. Granted, the family abode brings back memories, but not the anticipation it once solicited. "Never thought my heart could be so yearny," the lyrics continue. "Why did I decide to roam? Gonna take a sentimental journey, sentimental journey home."

Heaven is ultimately home. "In my father's house are many rooms," Jesus alerted his disciples; "if it were not so, I would have told you. I am going there to prepare a placer for you. And if I go and prepare a place for you, I will come back and take you to be with me that you also may be where I am" (John 14:2–3).

"I am torn between the two," Paul admits; "I desire to depart and be with Christ, which is better by far, but it is more necessary for you that I remain in the body" (Phil. 1:23). It was for him a win/win situation. Still, it was *better by far* to be going home. "Got my bags; got my reservation. Spent each dime I could afford. Like a child with wild anticipation, want to hear that 'all aboard.'"

There are times when this old body protests that I get to thinking how it was to be going home. Then, that warm, fuzzy feeling returns. I try to imagine the love welcoming me. It is not an altogether futile effort because I experienced the love of my parents upon my return from service.

I have heard it said that war is hell. Well, not actually. But perhaps it is the closest we come to it in this life. In contrast, home seemed to me like a return to sanity. My parents could not make everything right after so much had gone wrong, but God can and will. Heaven is ultimately home.

* * *

It is as we glorify God that we experience pleasure in its fullest extent. I have touched on this topic in one connection or another from time to time. It remains to pull loose ends together.

"In everything I did," Paul reminds the Ephesians elders, "I showed you that by this kind of hard work we must help the weak, remembering the words the Lord Jesus himself said, 'It is more blessed to give than to receive'" (Acts 20:35). In this regard, he modeled the Jewish ideal concerning vocation. It consisted of two aspects. First, one should be industrious. "Go to the ant, you sluggard," the sage admonished; "consider its ways and be wise!" (Prov. 6:6)

Is there no drudgery associated with labor? Yes, as consequent of the fall. Originally, it was a fulfilling experience. Ultimately, it will be so.

Second, one should be generous. Jesus told a story concerning a rich man whose land brought forth a bumper crop. "What shall I do?" he thought to himself. "I have no place to store my crops" (Luke 12:17). It apparently never occurred to him that he might share with those who were in need without the necessities of life.

After this, he concluded: "This Is what I will do. I will tear down my barns and build bigger ones, and there I will store all my grain and my goods. And I'll say to myself 'Take life easy; eat, drink and be merry.'" At this, God said to him: "you fool! This very night your life will be demanded from you. Then who will get what you prepared for yourself?" "This is how it will be with anyone who stores up things for himself," Jesus concluded, "but is not rich toward God."

Note the contrast between what the rich man anticipated and what actually transpired. He imagined that he would have time to squander his riches on himself; he did not survive the night. His pleasures were short lived.

Not so those who are rich toward God. Their pleasure multiplies with the passing of time. God is no person's debtor. He gives lavishly.

It begins now, in this life, and extends beyond the veil. "You prepare a table before me in the presence of my enemies," the psalmist enthuses. "You anoint my head with oil; my cup overflows. Sure goodness and love will follow me all the days of my life, and I will dwell in the house of the Lord forever" (23:5–6).

Forever is not something one can measure in time. In this life, every tick of the clock brings us closer to demise. In the future life, there will be no clocks. *Pleasure* is for now a fleeting experience. Not so in heaven! It will serve as a constant companion. Some pleasures better anticipate heaven than others. All things Considered, listen for the whispers of heaven.

All Things Considered

ALL THINGS CONSIDERED, THE discussion has focused on four divine mandates. Initially, however, we touched on their realm. Since it is critical to bear in mind that they originate with God, as the sovereign ruler of the universe. Who assuredly is eminently worthy of our reverence.

This expressly recalls the graphic imagery of Isaiah's encounter with the Almighty. "In the year that King Uzziah died, I saw the Lord seated on a throne high and exalted," the prophet allows, "and the train of his robe filled the temple" (Isa. 6:1). "Uzziah/Azariah died between 742 and 735 B.C. after an outstanding, prosperous 52-year reign and a period of regency with his son Jotham but leaving Assyrian storm clouds on the horizon."[1] These two factors combined to create uncertainty, except for the realization that the Lord's sovereignty was undiminished.

Above him were seraphs, each with six wings. "With two wings they covered their faces, with two they covered their feet, and with two they were flying. And they were calling to one another: 'Holy, holy, holy is the Lord Almighty, the whole earth is full of his glory.' At the sound of their voices the doorposts and thresholds shook and the temple was filled with smoke."

With two they covered their faces, as an awesome reminder of the divine glory. With two they covered their feet, lest they offend their Benefactor. And with two they flew, so as to attend to his wishes. While assuring one another that God's glory is reflected in creation.

"Woe to me!" Isaiah cried out. "I am ruined! For I am a man of unclean lips, and I live among a people of unclean lips, and my eyes have seen

---

1. Goldingway, *Isaiah*, 58.

the King, the Lord Almighty." As an unholy creature in the presence of a holy mentor.

Then one of the seraphs flew to him with a live coal in his hand, which he had taken with tongs from the altar. "See, this has touched your lips, your guilt is taken away and your sin is atoned for," the seraph informed him. Holiness does not preclude forgiveness. Nor that one whose lips were cleansed declare God's word.

Then Isaiah overheard the Lord inquire, "Whom shall I send? And who will go for us?" As if in deliberation with his attendants.

"Here am I," Isaiah volunteered. "Send me!" apparently caught up in the flow of events, and wishing to be involved.

Whereupon, he was enjoined to go and tell this people: "Be ever hearing, but never understanding; be ever seeing, but never perceiving. Make the hearts of this people calloused; make their ears dull and close their eyes. Otherwise they might see with their eyes, hear with their ears, understand with their hearts, and turn and be healed." "They constitute a warning of where the people will find themselves unless they respond and turn."[2]

"For how long, O Lord?" the prophet inquires. Anticipating that the people that the people will eventually turn from their calloused ways.

"Until the cities lie ruined and without inhabitants," the Lord replies. Until they are carried away into exile. Until only the stump remains, with anticipation that there would be future growth.

Welcome to the real world, where "Righteousness exalts a nation, but sin is a disgrace to any people" (Prov. 14:34). Where divine counsel is not to be ignored, nor are humans meant to procrastinate. Where the divine mandates assume their rightful place of importance.

But what is the nature of a *mandate*? It is not simply a suggestion, worthy of consideration but not otherwise binding. If uncertain as how to proceed, pray for guidance. Then, act accordingly, and refine one's efforts in the light of ensuing experience. Take a hands-on approach.

Which brings to mind the tine when Gideon was visited by an angel of the Lord. "The Lord be with you, mighty warrior," the heavenly visitor greeting him (Judg. 6:12). It appeared as if a call to decisive action. By way of providing leadership, and the renewing of the Israelite society.

"But sir," Gideon protested, "if the Lord is with us, why has all this happened to us? Where are all his wonders that our fathers told us about when they said, 'Did not the Lord bring us up out of Egypt?' But now the

---

2. Ibid., 61.

Lord has abandoned us and put us into the hand of Midian." As if God had failed them, whereas the reverse was true.

"Go with the strength you have," he was enjoined, and the Lord would be with him. "I tell you the truth," Jesus assured his disciples in this regard, "if you have faith as small as a mustard seed, you can say to this mountain, 'Move from here to there' and it will move. Nothing will be impossible for you" (Matt: 17:20). Allowing, in turn, for the dual admonition, "Expect great things from God, and undertake great things in his name."

Having explored the realm of divine mandates, we turned to *the paper trail*. This consisted of a brief survey of both Old and New Testaments, along with three pertinent case studies. Providing an extended context for a more pointed consideration of the divine mandates. In keeping with the sage reminder, "A text without its context is a pretext."

Biblical narrative consists of event plus privileged interpretation. Something happened to an individual or group on a given occasion. What can be learned from this? What was the divine intent in recording it? Failing to learn from the past, we are destined to relive its tragic consequences.

Yet, we are assuredly drawn toward the future. As revealed in Holy Writ. Providing caution and encouragement. Time with eternity in view.

Nevertheless, we act in the present. For better and for worse. "Do not boast about tomorrow," the sage enjoins, "for you do not know what a day may bring forth" (Prov. 27:1). Assume responsibility, and tomorrow's options will be greatly improved.

The paper trail comprises both continuity and discontinuity. As for continuity, "Let us hold unswervingly to the hope we profess, for he who promised is faithful" (Heb. 10:23). Whether evident in the course of events or not. As confirmed by the patriarchs, prophets, and apostles.

In more general terms, "Generations come and generations go, but the earth remains forever. The sun rises and the sun sets, and hurries back to where it rises. The wind blows to the south and turns to the north, round and round it goes, ever returning to its course." (Eccles. 1:4–6). And so on. "What has been will be again, what has been done will be done again; there is nothing new under the sun."

As for discontinuity, no two days are the same. Nor are any two persons the same. "Some faced jeers and flogging, while still others were chained and put in prison. They went about in sheepskins and goatskins, destitute, persecuted and mistreated—the world was not worthy of them. They wandered in deserts and mountains and in caves and holes in the

The Divine Mandates

ground" (Heb. 11:36–38). These were commended for their faith, and yet none of them received what has been promised. "God had planned something better for us so that only together with us would they be made perfect." Continuity and discontinuity coupled together in realistic fashion.

As noted above, the paper trail continues with three case studies. The first consisted of a brief visit with the apostolic fathers. Such as were thought to have been personally acquainted with one or more of the apostles. Consequently, bent on preserving the truths committed to the apostolic circle.

In particular, we considered Clement of Rome's representative *The epistle to the Corinthians* and the *Didarche*. After an accolade of praise, Clement addresses the problems faced by the congregation as a faithful mentor of the apostolic tradition. Conversely, the *Didarche* served as a church manual. It consisted of a moral treatise concerning the two ways, and a guide for church practices—the latter in anticipation of discussing the church mandate.

The second case study considered the rise of Christian apologists during the second century. Arguing that Christians should not be persecuted, and answering the charges brought against them. Selecting Justin Martyr as a spokesman.

Justin passionately appealed to reason as a mitigating factor. He thus hoped to establish a common ground from which to temper the vicious attacks against the Christian fellowship. Again with expressed bearing on the church mandate.

The final case study was of much more recent derivation. Serving as a reminder that Christian martyrdom is not simply a thing of the past. In fact, it is said that more Christians perished for their faith in the past century than all the previous centuries combined.

While Bonhoeffer's *The Cost of Discipleship* proved to be his most memorable work, associated with his imprisonment and execution, his *Ethics* expressly embraces the divine mandates. For instance, he reasons: "the divine mandates are introduced into the world from above as orders or 'institutions' of the reality of Christ, that is to say, of the reality of the love of God for the world and for men which is revealed in Jesus Christ. This means that they are not in any sense products of history; they are not earthy powers, but divine commissions."[3]

Given Bonhoeffer's attention to the divine mandates, this serves as a helpful transition into a more detailed discussion. The labor mandate first

---

3. Bonhoeffer, *Ethics*, 288.

invited our attention. As noted in this regard, "The Lord God took the man and put him in the garden of Eden to work it and take care of it" (Gen. 2:15). We are thus alerted to the fact that meaningful labor was intended to be fulfilling.

Recalling the interchange between two neighbors. The one observed that his friend could greatly increase his production through means available. The other appeared disinterested. "Why would I want to do that?" he inquired.

"So you can better provide for your family," the other observed. When this did not seem to suffice, he added: "So you can retire with ease."

I can do that now," the other replied. While content to do as little as thought necessary. Quite oblivious as to the positive character of labor.

Of course, labor took on negative implications with the fall. After which, humans would struggle with adverse circumstances. So that persons' experiences encounter the labor mandate from the perspective of the interim between paradise lost and regained.

Yet with the encouragement that persons heartily assume responsibility as an act of devotion. Thus to not only care for one's own needs, but that of those in dire need. Thereby coupling generosity with industry.

The discussion concludes with a brief discussion of recreation. As a desirable respite from one's labors, but not a substitute. While drawing on Tertullian and Hippolytus for their appraisal of the Roman games.

The family mandate next captures our attention. As with the labor mandate, it arises in context of the creation narrative. Wherein the Lord provides a suitable helper for Adam. Which allowed for their essential equality, while preserving their complimentary character.

Such laid stress on the marriage in terms of commitment. In ideal terms, until death should part the couple. Leaving a cherished legacy to those born of their union.

The vows are recited before God, thus affirming a sacred obligation. The ceremony is no less social for that reason, given those in attendance. Nor is it less interpersonal, involving the couple in an intimate relationship.

A situation is which the children are obligated to honor their parents. Implying obedience and respect. Moreover, to care for their parent's needs, especially during their declining years. Then to accord them fitting memorials: in ritual manner—as with a proper burial, with appreciative remembrance, and by incorporating their parental instruction.

The Divine Mandates

In historical perspective, the extended family looms large on the horizon. In more recent times, the nuclear family has taken on increased significance. As a result of great social mobility and diversity. Still more recently, alternatives have proliferated. As most notably with the single parent family.

This invited a consideration of fifteen recent developments that have impacted significantly on the family mandate. Such as the availability of birth control, exposure of erotic stimuli, and delay of marriage for educational purposes. The combined effect being to threaten the family as the basic building block of society.

Recalling the graphic imagery: "The hand which rocks the cradle rules the world."

The government mandate emerges in turn. Initially, this involved what was designated as *incipient government*. Such as dates from when humans begin to proliferate, and before the rise of regional authority structures. The latter is evidenced in the evolving of local governance in ancient Egypt, followed by its adaptation to a unified state.

The process can also be traced with the Israelites. At first, with the call of Abraham. Which envisaged a chosen people, set apart to intercede on behalf of others. Then with the Mosaic Covenant, establishing the conditions by which their role could be cultivated. Along with blessings and cursings, depending on their faithfulness. And allowing for a covenant renewal, which would provide continuity within change.

With the passing of time, the Israelites would negotiate the turbulent time of the judges. During which they would fall away, experience oppression, cry out to God and be delivered, only to repeat the pattern.

The monarchy eventually came into being. As previously noted, it consisted of a complex system of checks and balances. Such as included the sovereign, school of the prophets, priestly establishment, wisdom tradition, and the general populace. But it was expressly the prophets that assumed the monumental task of fine-tuning the people to their covenant obligations.

There were also occasions when the chosen people were subject to the rule of alien authorities. Their bondage in Egypt especially comes to mind in this connection. So that they pled with the Lord in their distress, and he delivered them. So also with their exile, when they reflected: "By the rivers of Babylon we sat and wept when we remembered Zion" (Psa. 137:1). Likewise recalling the dramatic account of Daniel and his associates in a foreign land. Still later, the Jews were subject to Roman rule. Creating divisions with the populace, some more willing to accommodate than others.

Thus when Jesus was asked if one should pay Roman taxes, he replied: "Give to Caesar what is Caesar's and to God what is God's" (Matt. 22:21). Not that these are separate, let alone equal domains. But rather that the government mandate prevails.

Paul confirms that government is ordained by God, although not all that eventuates is approved by him. Consequently, submission is as a rule approved. But not if it violates matters of conscience.

This discussion concludes with three pertinent case studies. The first was of more abstract nature, dealing with alternative models for political engagement. The second provocatively explored Irenaeus' political discourse. While the third took a more practical approach, with the opportunities for voluntary service.

The church mandate rounded out the consideration of particular mandates. In this regard, there is a pronounced continuity in salvation history. Such as originates with Adam and recast with Noah, as pertains to Abraham and Moses, as expressed by the prophets, and climaxed with Jesus and the apostles. So whereas in a strict sense of relatively recent derivation, actually with a long and venerable tradition.

In particular, the church is characterized as *apostolic*. In keeping with the observation that the early followers of Jesus "devoted themselves to the apostles' teaching" (Acts 2:42). As set forth in the New Testament compilation.

If apostolic, then likewise *holy*. "Don't you know that you yourselves are God's temple, and that God's Spirit lives in you?" Paul pointedly inquires. "If anyone destroys God's temple, God will destroy him; for God's temple is sacred, and you are that temple" (1 Cor. 3:16–17).

If apostolic, finally *universal*. As alluded to above, "whether Jews or Greeks, slave or free." Suggesting that every culture may be employed for the purpose of heralding the gospel, while none is pristine. Thus contributing to unity, when understood as constructive diversity.

This chapter then concludes with a relatively brief discussion of the institutional character of the church. Such as is meant to preserve the dynamic concept of the church as mandate. As a vibrant community, free from legalistic constraint.

It goes without saying that God provides the means for what he desires humans to accomplish. So it is that divine endowments correlate with

The Divine Mandates

mandates. As for the former, we explored life, liberty, and the pursuit of happiness.

As for *life*, Job observed: "the Lord gave and the Lord has taken away, may the name of the Lord be praised" (Job 1:22). Which earned him the chronicle's commendation, "In all this, Job did not sin by charging God with wrongdoing." Conversely, those who inexcusably take life usurp the divine prerogative.

Our attention was first called to the tree of life to which humans would have had access if it had not been for violating the injunction of the Lord. Then to Cain's wrongful death of his sibling. Subsequently with Noah's deliverance from the deluge.

Afterward, with the agitation for population control. Especially as illustrated by the commons, and crowded lifeboat analogies. Extending into the issue of abortion, and concluding with thoughts concerning terrorism.

As for *liberty*, humans were born free. Free to serve God and too minister to one another. However, they chose self-indulgence, and thereby lost their divine leverage. This eventually led to the Israelite bondage in Egypt, designated earlier *as the seventh falling away*—depicting its depth of degradation.

The topic was expanded by way of three case studies. These concerned the role of prayer in revival, church and state relations, and an appeal for religious tolerance. Prayer first so as to involve the Lord in the quest for liberty.

Repeated for emphasis, Jesus declared: "So if the Son sets you free, you will be free indeed" (John 8:36). If in physical bondage, then free in spirit. Hence, freed indeed!

As for *the pursuit of happiness*, this does not serve as a guarantee. Some prove to be more successful than others. And some are more inhibited than others. But humans were meant to enjoy life.

Blessed amounts to a near equivalent, although the accent appears to be more along the line of an objective appraisal. Consequently, a person who finds wisdom in considered blessed, since it is more precious than silver or gold. So also the person who keeps divine instruction. Likewise, one who trust in the Lord.

This invited a consideration of the beatitudes. Such as those who cultivate peace, or are persecuted for righteousness. As an encouragement to Jesus' disciples, in the presence of the multitude.

Then, including with essays illustrative of *whispers of heaven*, otherwise described as *enduring pleasure*. As in the instances of scaling a mountain, and returning home after overseas military duty. Along with the assurance that the best is yet to come. Thus fortifying one's commitment to the divine mandates.

Bibliography

American Baptist Churches in the U.S.A. "Policy Statement on Family Life."
Bagatti, Bellarmino. *The Church of the Circumcision*. Jerusalem: Franciscan, 1971.
Baldwin, Joyce. *Esther*. Downers Grove: Inter-Varsity, 1984.
Bauman, Michael and David Hall (eds.). *God & Caesar*. Camp Hall: Christian Publications, 1994.
Bethge, Eberhard. *Dietrich Bonhoeffer*. New York: Harper & Row, 1970.
Bingham, D. Jeffrey. "Irenaeas and the Kingdoms of the World." In *God & Caesar* Bauman and Hall (eds.), 27–40.
Bonhoeffer, Dietrich. *The Cost of Discipleship*. New York: Macmillan, 1963.
———. *Ethics*. New York: Macmillan, 1965.
———. *Life Together*. New York: Harper & Row, 1954.
Bruce, F. F. *The Book of the Acts*. Grand Rapids: Eerdmans, 1988.
Buzzard, Lynn. "Separation of Church, State, and Religious Liberty" *Christian Citizens* (Land & Moore, eds.), 32–46.
Carr, Steven & Franklin Meyer. *Celebrate Life*. Brentwood: Wolgemuth & Hyatt, 1990.
Center For Defense Information. *A Brief History of Terrorism*.
Chapman, Morris. "Kneel Down and Be Counted" *Christian Citizens* (Land & Moore, eds.), 11–22.
Clement of Alexandria. *The Stromata*.
Clorfene, Chaim and Yazov Rogalsky. *The Path of the Righteous Gentile*. Southfield: Targum, 1987.
Cole, R. Alan. *Exodus*. Downers Grove: Inter-Varsity, 1973.
Colson, Charles and Nancy Pearce. *How Shall I Live?* Wheaton: Tyndale, 1999.
Cullmann, Oscar. "Immortality of the Soul or Resurrection of the Dead," *Immortality and Resurrection* (Stendal, ed.), 9–53.
Didarche.
Dulles, Avery. *Models of the Church*. New York: Doubleday, 1978.
The Epistle of Clement to the Corinthians.
The Epistle to Diognetus.
Estes, David. "Psalm 101 and the Ethics of Political Leadership" *God & Caesar* (Bauman and Hall, eds.), 7–25.
Evans, Mary. *1 and 2 Samuel*. Peabody: Hendrickson, 2003.

Bibliography

Fee, Gordon. *The First Epistle to the Corinthians*. Grand Rapids: Eerdmans, 1987.
Goldingay, John. *Isaiah*. Peabody: Hendrickson, 2001.
Guthrie, Donald. *The Pastoral Epistles*. Grand Rapids: Eerdmans, 1992.
Green, Joel. *The Gospel of Luke*. Grand Rapids: 1997.
Hamilin, E. John. *Judges: At Risk in the Promised Land*. Grand Rapids: Eerdmans, 1990.
Harris, J., C. Brown, and M. Moore. *Joshua, Judges, Ruth*. Peabody: Hendrickson, 2003.
Hartley, John. *Genesis*. Peabody: Hendrickson, 2003.
Henry, Carl F. H. "Religious Liberty As a Cause Celebre" *Christian Citizens* (Land & Moore, eds.), 64–77.
Heschel, Abraham. *The Prophets*. Peabody: Prince, 2001.
Hess, Richard. *Joshua*. Downers Grove: Inter-Varsity, 1996.
Hoffmeier, James (ed.). *Abortion: A Christian Understanding and Response*. Grand Rapids: Baker, 1987.
———. "Abortion and the Old Testament Law," *Abortion* (Hoffmeier, ed.), 49–63.
Humanist Manifesto 1.
Inch, Morris. *The Enigma of Justice*. Eugene: Wipf & Stock, 2010.
———. *Scripture As Story*. Lanham: University Press of America, 2000.
———. *Thumbs Up For the Family*. Durham: Eloquent, 2010.
———. *Understanding Bible Prophecy*. New York: Harper & Row, 1977.
———. *Whispers of Heaven & Heaven According to Matthew*. Fairfax: Xulon, 2002.
———. *Why Take the Church Seriously?* Baltimore: PublishAmerica, 1985.
Irenaeus. *Against Heresies*.
The Joint Declaration of the Doctrine of Justification.
Justin Martyr. *The First Apology*.
———. *The Second Apology*.
Kaiser, Walter, Jr. *Toward Old Testament Ethics*. Grand Rapids: Academia Books, 1983.
Kelly, John. *Early Christian Creeds*. London: Logmans, 1960.
Kidner, Derek. *Genesis*. Downers Grove: Inter-Varsity, 1967.
Klein, Ralph. *Israel in Exile: A Theological Interpretation*. Philadelphia: Westminster, 1979.
Land, Richard & Louis Moore (eds.). *Citizens Christians*. Nashville: Broadman & Holman, 1994.
Lane, Tony. *Exploring Christian Thought*. Nashville: Thomas Nelson, 1996.
Latourette, Kenneth Scott. *A History of Christianity*. New York: Harper & Brothers, 1953.
Lightfoot, J. B. *The Apostolic Fathers*. Grand Rapids: Baker, 1967.
The Martyrdom of the Holy Martyrs.
Melton, J. Gordon. *The Churches Speak on Sex and Family Life*. Detroit: Gale Research, 1991.
Moo, Douglas. *The Epistle to the Romans*. Grand Rapids: Eerdmans, 1996.
Morris, Leon. *1 Corinthians*. Downers Grove: Inter-Varsity, 1990.
———.. *The First and Second Epistles to the Thessalonians*. Grand Rapids: Eerdmans, 1991.
Mounce, Robert. *The Book of Revelation*. Grand Rapids: Eerdmans, 1977.
———. *Matthew*. Peabody: Hendrickson, 1991.
Musurillo, Herbert. *The Fathers of the Primitive Church*. New York: Mentor-Omega, 1966.
The One Year Book of Hymns. Wheaton: Tyndall, 1995.
Orr, Robert, David Shieldermayer, and David Biebel. *Life and Death Decisions*. Colorado Springs: NavPress, 1990.

Bibliography

Patai, Raphael. *Society, Culture and Change in the Middle East*. Philadelphia: University of Pennsylvania, 1971.
Patzia, Arthur. *Ephesians, Colossians, Philemon*. Peabody: Hendrickson, 1993.
Pfeiffer, Charles. *Old Testament History*. Grand Rapids: Baker, 1984.
Placher, William. *A History of Christian Theology*. Philadelphia: Westminster, 1983.
Potman, Louis. *Life and Death*. Mishawaka: Better World, 1992.
Pope Paul VI. "Human Vitae."
Routley, Erik. *Creeds and Confessions*. Philadelphia: Westminster, 1952.
Stack, Jay. "How Christians Can Have an Impact on Volunteers" *Citizen Christians* (Land & Moore, eds.), 128–136.
Stendal, Keister (ed.). *Immortality and Resurrection*. New York: Macmillan, 1965.
Sypes, Leon (ed.). *The Eternal Vision*. Peabody: Hendrickson, 2002.
Tertullian, *De Spectaculis*.
Thielicke, Helmut. *I Believe*. Philadelphia: Fortress, 1974.
The Universal Declaration of Human Rights.
Walton, John and Victor Matthews. *Genesis-Deuteronomy*. Downers Grove: InterVarsity, 1997.
Watkins, William. *The New Absolutes*. Minneapolis: Bethany, 1996.
Wenham, Gordon. *Genesis 1–15*. Dallas: Word, 1991.
Westerhoff, John III. *Living the Faith Community*. San Francisco: Harper & Row, 1985.
Williams, David. *Acts*. Peabody: Hendrickson, 1993.
Wilson, Marvin. *Our Father Abraham: Jewish Roots of the Christian Faith*. Grand Rapids: Eerdmans, 1989.
World Synod of Bishops. "Message to Christian Families."
Wright, Christopher. *Deuteronomy*. Peabody: Hendrickson, 2003.
Zimmermann, Wolf-Dieter and Ronald Smith (ed.). *I Knew Dietrich Bonhoeffer*. New York: Harper & Row, 1966.

www.ingramcontent.com/pod-product-compliance
Lightning Source LLC
Chambersburg PA
CBHW050815160426
43192CB00010B/1774